DO-OVER

*How God Turned My 30-Year
Mess Into A Message*

By

JOANNA THOMAS

DEDICATION

For Jesus, the Author and Finisher of our faith…
and our stories.

TABLE OF CONTENTS

ACKNOWLEDGEMENTS

First and foremost, all glory and honor goes to God. My life and this story wouldn't exist without Him. He gets all the credit for my gift as a writer, though in all honesty, the only real gift I bring to the table is that of being a good typist. He always has been, and always will be, the real Author of any story I write.

To my publishing team at Xulon Press: Thank you for helping make this dream a reality. I couldn't have done it without you!

To Veronica, my friend, editor and cheerleader: Thank you for lending your time, talent and enthusiasm to this project. Working with you made this book a true labor of love and I hope that this is just the first of many, such collaborations. I love you to the moon and back, Little Owl!

To Steve, my pastor and friend: Thank you for leading me to the Lord and for your discipleship all these years. I wouldn't be the Christ-follower I am today had you not been willing to pour into my life.

All of us at Graceway Christian Church are blessed to have you as our shepherd. You saw my writing gift, and this book, long before I did. Thank you for your encouragement to write it, and share it, and for your prayers all along the way.

To Ellen, my counselor and facilitator of healing: You walked with me during the lowest and most challenging points in my life, and helped me turn losses into lessons. Thank you for helping me plant stakes of wisdom during our 15 months together as we prepared my heart for God to lay a foundation of redemption and restoration.

To Susan, my friend and one of the wisest women I know: Thank you for your friendship and for giving me the final nudge to write this book, the one that got me listening to God so He could give me the outline for this story.

To my friends and family who read my blog and encourage me to continue writing: Your friendship and faithful readership are a blessing. Your presence pushes me to dig deeper into my faith and my relationship with God, and to improve my craft.

Finally, to all of my friends and family members who have walked this road with me: God placed each and every one of you in my life for a reason. Whether you walked with me across the highest peaks or through the lowest valleys, or both, your presence is a gift that I will always treasure. I love you all.

PREFACE

Don't forget – no one else sees the world the way you do, so no one else can tell the stories that you have to tell. **– Charles de Lint**

Last year, a good friend encouraged me to write and share my story. Her suggestion came on the heels of two other nudges from God prompting me to do the same. I went home after having dinner with my friend, and curled up on my bed with a journal and pen. "OK, God," I whispered, "You've been prompting me to write my story. I have no idea what to write or where to start, but I'm ready to listen and take notes." Immediately, God started to download ideas. Two hours later, I had 17 chapters outlined. It was a full-blown story of my life including $25,000 of debt, seven years of online dating addiction and sexual sin, three failed marriages, two lost careers, one prodigal journey, and God's redemption of it all.

Catherine Aird, a British crime novelist, is quoted as saying, "If you can't be a good example then you'll just have to be a horrible warning." After finishing this book, that quote seemed like the perfect tag line for my life. I'd been through so much, most of it due to foolish decisions and poor judgment. In the wake of those decisions, there was a path of wreckage over 30 years long and at the root of it all was a foundation of lies.

As a child, I believed I was an accident. I often felt like a mistake here in the world. Later, I believed that it wasn't okay to be who I really was. In young adulthood, I started believing that I would always have to settle in life and that I wasn't worthy of anything or anyone really great or special. Those lies would lead to others in my life, and they would direct my thinking and decision-making for three decades. It wouldn't be until the age of 46, after the end of my third marriage, that I would be broken enough to admit I was the common denominator in all of my trials and messes. If I wanted my life to be different, I first had to be willing to let God make *me* different.

Over a period of three and a half years, I submitted to God's painstaking and often painful handiwork as He stripped away the lies. Layer after layer, He peeled it all away and slowly began to replace it with His truth. That truth would become my new, unshakeable foundation in life and would open the door to a future characterized by wisdom, discernment, freedom and contentment.

In the aftermath of my mess, God has given me a message with the hope that others won't have to travel the same broken road as me. Perhaps you will see yourself in these pages and will recognize the same kinds of lies in your own life, and you will hear God whispering that it's time to make a change today. For those who have been on that road for some time already, my hope is that this book will encourage you and prove that it's never too late for a do-over in God's economy.

Rest assured that while this book relates events from my own life, the story is really God's. I pray that as you read about my brokenness, you will see God's grace; as you read about my failures, you will see God's redemption; as you read about my folly, you will see God's restoration; and as you read about my rebellion, you will see God's mercy. My prayer is that as you read about me, you will see God revealed in all His glory.

Joanna Thomas
February 2015

INTRODUCTION

—————»⊰ ❈ ⊱«—————

Imagine a woman. We'll call her "Woman A." She's gone out to pick up lunch one day, and in the process gets propositioned for a date by the gentleman chatting her up in line. It's the first time that's happened to her, so naturally she's flattered. When asked, she gives the gentleman her phone number and he promises to call and set up a date. After returning to her car, instead of immediately heading back to the office, she stops, drops and prays. Before she even starts her car or removes the sunshades, she bows her head and asks God for wisdom and discernment in the matter. This man she's just met is a total stranger and there is no way she could possibly know what she needs to in order to make a wise decision. But God does. She believes God's Word when He says that He sees the hearts of men and knows everything about them.[1] She trusts God to reveal great and mighty things she does not know when she takes the time to call upon Him.[2]

Because dating has been an area of extreme brokenness in her life, she has willingly embraced a dependence upon God to guide and lead her in this area. She has been seeking God and journaling as He speaks, so she is aware of patterns in her life and she sees that God is opening a new season before her. Understanding that this is a vulnerable time when the enemy would love to distract or derail her, she is alert to his schemes and lies. She thanks God in advance for the insight she knows He will provide and commits herself to waiting on God for His answers.

As the day progresses, she grows uneasy about her gentleman caller. He seemed to be a nice enough man but the Holy Spirit has been reminding her about something he said in their brief conversation. He was a contract worker, here in town from out of state. Perhaps he is married with a family in his home town. Maybe he is just looking for a little entertainment while he finishes up this job. She recalls an earlier time in her own life when she used to keep the company of married men and decides to heed what seems like cautioning from God. Later that afternoon, God whispers to her that she is no longer anyone's mistress and that she is His best for someone. His encouragement strengthens her identity in Christ and reinforces her unwillingness to settle for anything less than God's best in this life.

When her gentleman caller follows up that night and leaves a phone message, she chooses to again pray and ask for wisdom about how best to tell him that she has changed her mind and will be declining his invitation. The next morning, she returns the call and politely refuses the offer. Over the next two days, she receives a few text messages from him as he tries to change her mind. She remains steadfast and graciously declines the additional invites. In their phone call and in those text messages, she hears and sees phrases that immediately indicate red flags for her. Neediness and vacancy are apparent in his comments, along with a desire to be made complete by someone else. Not only that, she also sees his obvious refusal to honor the boundary she established in their phone conversation. She whispers a thank you to God for leading her to decline the invitation, seeing in his follow up comments proof that this gentleman wasn't the right one for her.

Now, imagine another woman. We'll call her "Woman B." This woman has set up an eHarmony account and has been responding to a variety of matches through the website. On this particular day, she has been matched up with a gentleman who looks really good on paper and lives 800 miles and two states away from her. Speeding through the guided communication process, they immediately start emailing one another directly. Less than a week later, before they have even spoken on the phone, he confesses he is falling in love with her. She has been praying for wisdom in the matter but she is not listening for God's reply. She engages in phone conversations with her suitor and soon they are talking multiple times throughout the day. He often calls her during her afternoon work hours, and while she would rather wait until after work, she takes his calls and text messages anyway. Their evening calls often keep her up later than she would like, but she rarely says anything for fear of turning him away.

In writing and over the phone, she is chatty and shares her life in tremendous detail. In response, he is vague and less than forthcoming with details about his own life. Nevertheless, the more she learns about him, the more she is convinced that he is "the one." He has told her how much he needs a woman in his life to take care of him and how his home needs a woman's touch. She begins to imagine all the ways she can improve his life. Two weeks into their communication, they begin to hint at marriage and make plans for their first face-to-face meeting.

A couple of weeks later, he travels to meet her and they arrange for her to visit him so they can get engaged. She sees him as the answer to many of her prayers and needs including security, companionship, and meaning in her life. One week later, she makes the first of only two trips to visit him and he proposes. She accepts and they rush through the remainder of their 4-month engagement. During that time, she notices behaviors that are somewhat disturbing but she is quick to make excuses for her fiancé. He works a high-stress job, she tells her friends. It's just difficult being 800 miles apart, she reasons to herself. Things will get better once we're married and I'm with him full-time.

They sign up for a pre-marital counseling class and rush through the homework as quickly as they did their online communication. It's just one more thing checked off the list so they can get married. In the process, though, he misses two of the six classes due to his work schedule and never listens to the make-up tapes or does the homework for those weeks.

His weekend visits to see her are spent together, just the two of them, because he has told her he doesn't want to take up the precious little time they have with social activities involving her friends. During the two visits she makes to see him, she never meets his friends, his coworkers or his two daughters. All that time alone creates ample opportunity to push the celibacy envelope. While she has clearly communicated her desire to wait until their wedding night for physical intimacy, she constantly has to remind him of her commitment in that area.

Almost 4 ½ months from the date they were matched on eHarmony, they get married. Two weeks later, she leaves her job of 7 ½ years, all of her friends and family, and a budding community service ministry at her church to move out of state and start her new life. She is absolutely convinced that she is following God into this new chapter of life despite not having received any biblical confirmation or wise counsel from godly friends.

Two different women? Yes and no. "Woman A" is me; so is "Woman B."

Four years, almost to the day, separate the two experiences described above. What happened during those four years to transform a fear-filled, naïve, relationally-stunted, codependent, mask-wearing, boundary-less, thinking-she-had-it-all-together Christian woman into a broken, humbled, transparent, faith-filled, dependent, knowing-she-doesn't-have-it-all-together follower of Christ? The answer isn't a what; it's a Who. Jesus happened to me and when He showed up, He led me on a journey into my past. Along the way, we dug up treasures and uncovered truth. We made a lot of trips to the emotional dump. We let go of lies. We rescinded spiritual and emotional agreements. We broke unhealthy soul ties. We walked a long, hard road but we walked it *together*.

However, before we can unpack those four years of healing and transformation, we have to go back and look at how it all started because addiction is a funny thing. It doesn't just happen. It usually starts off simply and surreptitiously. The beginning of an addiction seems almost innocent and harmless; by the time you realize you have a problem, it's too late. At that point, you're in over your head and it's almost impossible to climb out of that pit.

My own online dating addiction started long before I met my third husband in 2010. We have to go back to 1997, when my first marriage was ending because of *my husband's* online addiction.

Chapter 1

32/F/S

It was Presidents' Day weekend 1997 and I'd gone to my parents' to help them prepare their taxes. My husband had stayed home to rest and when I returned I found him on the computer. That in itself wasn't unusual. We, along with the rest of the country, had jumped on board the internet bandwagon. America Online was pretty much the only game in town at the time and we had signed up for an account the previous year. "Don" was constantly on the computer, visiting chat rooms and instant messaging people. He would sometimes share snippets from those conversations, telling me about the various and sundry friends he was making online all across the nation. Early on, it just seemed to be an electronic community of pen pals and it didn't concern me much.

But Don started to spend more and more time online during our last year of marriage. We both worked day jobs but in the evenings he would usually disappear into the spare bedroom and spend hours at the computer. I wasn't much of a night owl and would often call it a night by 10:00. My husband usually didn't crawl into bed until well after midnight.

They often say that a woman whose husband is cheating on her senses it long before she actually discovers the infidelity. They say that because it's true. As our last year together progressed, I sensed something had shifted in our relationship. Things had been deteriorating for a while but the last year saw an increase in tension and a decrease in connection. We rarely spent time together. When we did, it was only to take care of essential household business or family matters.

Driving home that afternoon, I still couldn't really put my finger on what was wrong; I just knew that he was keeping secrets and that the key to it all was on our computer. I got home and walked in to the bedroom to say hello. As I stepped up to where he was sitting, an instant message window popped up on the screen. "Can't let her see you here?" All of the fear, tension and frustration which had been building up for months suddenly snapped. I no longer cared about being polite and I was no longer afraid of the confrontation that I always knew would have to happen.

An avalanche of questions came pouring out of my mouth, but the only one I can recall clearly is "Who is she?" His immediate reply cut me to the quick: "She's my new best friend." For 11 years I had been his closest friend and confidant. Suddenly, I had been replaced by a single mother of three small children in North Carolina. I honestly don't know what hurt me more in that moment—the betrayal itself or the fact that it had happened under my roof while I was sleeping in the next bedroom.

In the months and years that followed, I often thought about that moment and about how men and women process infidelity differently. For men, I think the physical betrayal is what cuts the deepest. Thinking about their wife in the arms of another man is probably a picture they replay in their minds over and over again. For women, I think the emotional betrayal is harder. Hearing my own husband tell me that he had a new best friend was devastating; it absolutely crushed me. I'd spent the prior year pretty much alone in the marriage only to find out that my husband had been engaged in lengthy and intimate online conversations with a woman 3,000 miles away. Rejection like that was hard enough, but to later have him refuse marriage counseling simply added insult to injury. I wasn't wanted *and* I wasn't worthy of a fight to save our marriage.

In the midst of all that shock, there was still a part of me that wanted — actually needed — to know how this had all happened. What was so appealing about the chat rooms? How did instant messaging work? What kind of people spent hours online talking to strangers across the country? After my husband moved out that week, I began going through the computer files and found logs which had recorded his time online. He had been spending 7-8 hours a day using his AOL account. I started doing the math: eight hours a day at work, eight hours a day online, plus a few hours thrown in for sleeping and commuting. It was no wonder our marriage had fallen apart.

Because I worked all day in an office, the last thing I ever wanted to do was come home and sit in front of a computer, but that's exactly what I started doing. I signed up for my own AOL account and I started visiting chat rooms. Initially, my intention was simply to see what my husband had found so interesting and to get an idea of the types of people who hung out in chat rooms. I went into things with an obviously biased attitude, considering the circumstances. Angry and hurt, I visited the chat rooms with a major chip on my shoulder. I was almost looking to pick a fight, just waiting for any opportunity to make a snarky remark and tear someone apart. Any woman I ended up chatting with wasn't a potential friend; she was Ms. North Carolina. Any man who dared send me an instant message was instantly the enemy, nothing more than another unhappy husband looking for some "innocent" fun.

The Bible says we are not to let anger take root in our heart, for if we do then the enemy can gain a foothold.[3] I was so angry in the wake of my husband's infidelity. The more I nurtured that anger with my online escapades, the deeper in I was drawn. My heart was broken wide open and the enemy began speaking all kinds of lies to me. In the aftermath of rejection and being ignored, chat rooms provided an environment where I could be noticed and pursued. Suddenly finding myself alone for the first time in my life, chat rooms provided companionship and recreation each evening after work. Not having dated before I met my husband, I wasn't prepared to actually meet new people. Chat rooms were a safe and protected playground where I could explore and experiment without physical consequence. Instead of dealing with what had happened and processing through my hurt, I escaped into chat rooms and used them to self-medicate.

Eventually, the anger gave way to fascination. In chat rooms, I was 32/F/S: a 32-year-old single female. I wasn't rejected or neglected. I wasn't in the midst of a difficult and contentious divorce. I could be whoever I wanted: brazenly flirtatious, coy and demure, erudite and scholarly, or witty and sharp-tongued. Having learned the lingo, I became proficient at chatting and it wasn't uncommon for me to participate in as many as six separate instant message conversations at once.

I was spending more and more time online at night. I couldn't wait to get home, fix a plate of food, then plop down in front of the computer and spend the entire evening bouncing around chat rooms. At work, I would think about some of the people I'd met online and began to look forward to seeing them in the chat rooms we frequented. I viewed them as friends despite never having met and they even started to become more important than my own family. Without even realizing it, I was becoming addicted.

It begs the question: Are we hard-wired in our brain for addiction? Or, does the perfect storm of life circumstances have to come together for us to become addicted to something or someone? It's the age-old debate of nature vs. nurture. That's a bigger discussion for someone smarter than me to facilitate but since I'm just telling my own story here, let me say that the stage was set very early on for me—at my conception.

Chapter 2
AN ADDICT IS BORN

In *The Purpose Driven Life*, Rick Warren tells his readers that they are not an accident.[4] In fact, he spends an entire chapter driving home that particular point. I still remember how I cried uncontrollably the first time I read the poem at the end of that chapter. For the first time in my life, at the age of 43, there was another reality to consider: the fact that I had value and worth simply because God created me and put me here in the world. Up until that time, I had been believing and living a lie.

My parents met in San Francisco in the early sixties. My mom and grandma had moved there from a wide spot in the road in Northern California at the base of Mt. Shasta. Mom was the quieter and more sheltered of the two girls in her family, and still being single in her early 30s, she was the one my grandma accompanied when she ventured out into the world. My dad was newly divorced, his wife having left him to return to her family of origin. She had taken their two children with her and left him to start over in life. He drove west and when he ended up at the Pacific Ocean, he figured he'd gone as far as he could from Georgia and took up residence there.

They both ended up working at The Wall Street Journal in downtown San Francisco. My dad worked in the newsroom and monitored the news ticker machine; mom worked in the Personnel department. Dad loved to tell the story of when he first met my mom. He had been sent upstairs to Personnel to complete some paperwork. When he first walked through the double doors, my mom's back was to him. Hearing someone come in, she turned around, flashed a brilliant smile, and greeted my dad. He was instantly smitten. For my dad, it was love at first sight; less so for my mom. The way she used to tell it, my dad asked her out repeatedly and she kept refusing. She finally said yes because she felt sorry for him and felt like she owed him a date after all that asking.

I'm not sure how long they had been dating before my mom got pregnant with me, but for a 34-year-old Catholic, Hispanic virgin, no amount of time would have been enough to justify her behavior in the eyes of my grandma. My parents got married primarily because my grandma forced the issue. She told my mom, "You liked him enough to sleep with him. You'll like him enough to marry him." My grandma had spoken and that was that. It would be many decades before I'd realize what a blessing God had given me in my grandma. Had she not been there to fight for me, it's unlikely I would have been born.

As a child, I often heard the story about my parents' dating and my unexpected arrival. "You were an accident," they'd say. My mom always stressed the part about how my grandma brought pressure to bear in the matter, as if she still resented it all those years later. I once asked my mom straight out if she would have married my dad and had kids if she hadn't gotten pregnant with me. It's one of those questions that nags at you, but once you have the answer you regret having asked. My mom clearly hadn't been in love with my dad and she had never really pursued the life she had desired. She told me she didn't really know, but it was the things she didn't say that spoke volumes. It was obvious that had she not been so tightly under her mother's influence, she might have made different choices in life. Like I said, I kind of regretted having asked the question in the first place.

It's tough to hear that you weren't really wanted; tougher yet to have it be the running family joke while growing up. Every year on my birthday, my parents would wish me a happy birthday and I'd wish them a happy anniversary. They had gotten married in February 1964, shortly after finding out they were pregnant, then had a church wedding on my birthday in September — except it wasn't supposed to be my birthday. I was about three weeks early and my arrival cut the reception short. The most celebrated thing about me as a child was my unexpected arrival and my accidental presence in this world.

That inauspicious start to my life would have ripple effects into my forties. I spent most of my life apologizing for taking up space in the world. I can still picture how I used to respond when accidentally bumping into someone in a store: physically shrinking into myself, feeling as if I'd committed some horrible offense for being in the same spot as someone else, like I shouldn't have been there in the first place. In my late thirties, during a brief stint at a hypnotherapy school, I went through a rebirthing exercise which included some regression hypnosis. During that session, we uncovered a lot of anger towards my mom. At the time, I was mad that she had gone through with the pregnancy and brought me into this world, unwanted. However, now knowing the truth about God's gift of life and having worked through past hurts in my life, I know it wasn't the pregnancy itself that angered me; not being wanted had been the real problem and that knowledge contributed to a lifetime of poor decisions and foolish behavior.

Childhood wouldn't do much to address this poor entrance into life. As a matter of fact, it would just compound the issue.

When asked about my upbringing, I used to tell people that I had a very "utilitarian" childhood; that may seem like an odd word to use but it was appropriate. In essence, my basic needs were met. My parents stayed married, my dad was always employed, and they made a comfortable home for us. They made sure my sister and I stayed in school and grew up to be responsible members of society.

Norman Rockwell probably wouldn't have found much to paint about in our family: no cuddling up together for stories at bedtime, no long walks together to just talk and share our day, and no mother/daughter or even father/daughter date nights. It's not that there wasn't *any* affection; it's just that we related to one another more out of our heads than our hearts. We reasoned and we discussed. We took care of business and kept things neat and tidy, emotionally-speaking. We lived on the surface of life and never delved into deep waters.

I don't think it was always that way for my family. When I was still small, I remember a very loud and intense fight between my parents. I don't recall the subject of the disagreement but my parents were sitting on the couch facing one another, with my mom finally getting in my dad's face saying, "You want to hit me? Go ahead!" My sister and I had been holed up with my grandma in the kitchen but at that point, I ran out into the living room and yelled at both of them to stop fighting. They sent me back into the kitchen and eventually resolved the issue. I never heard or saw my parents argue like that again.

I believe my parents were both people of great passion; the argument I witnessed testified to that, but through circumstances in life they learned to turn down that flame. They let life extinguish their light and I only got to see a faint glimmer of who God had made them to be. Perhaps my dad just grew up too fast, having become a parent to his younger siblings because of an absent mom and financial poverty. Maybe my mom just gave up after fighting her iron-willed mother for so many years and hearing one too many comparisons to her younger sister. Whatever the reason, they both turned into mere shadows of their true selves and they parented me and my sister from that place. Their influence would end up cementing a life-altering event near the end of my fifth-grade year.

Before the fifth grade, I was a pretty precocious child having inherited my parents' true passion for life. I was fearless and outgoing and didn't worry about what others thought of me. In first grade, I was in love with a little boy named Doug. His slicked-back hair, freckles, and gap-toothed smile were too much for me to resist. At our school open house that year, I sought out Doug, grabbed his hand, walked him over to my dad, and boldly introduced him, "Dad, Doug. Doug, Dad." In second grade, I ran for Student Body Council and made a campaign speech in front of an auditorium full of kids and faculty. In early fifth grade, I tried out for the cheerleading squad. I had absolutely no concept that I couldn't do something. If I was interested in it, I went for it.

School and learning were two things I loved at that age. I enjoyed sitting in the front row and I always raised my hand when I knew the answer to a question. I never held back or worried about how I came across until the end of my fifth-grade year. For some reason, the two girls who sat behind me that year decided they'd had enough of the smart girl in the front row. They would whisper and giggle behind me and eventually began to spray the back of my head with a little plastic water ring. That was the year I first got pegged with the term "Teacher's Pet."

If you've ever been teased in school, you understand the dilemma. On the one hand, you desperately want the teasing to stop. Yet you also harbor this weird desire to still be liked by the very same kids who are harassing you. Do you tell on them? Or do you stay quiet?

Instead of confronting the behavior, I chose to do what my own parents had done. I became smaller. I became less. In that fifth-grade classroom, I didn't just learn English and Math; I learned to become invisible in the world and to stifle who I really was. I still loved learning but I stopped letting people know it—no more sitting in the front row or raising my hand every time I knew the answer. I stopped engaging with life and with people in a genuine and authentic way. If being yourself got you harassed, I reasoned, then I'd be whoever I needed to be in order to be liked. That's when I learned to be a chameleon.

I became the good student and the good daughter; "good" meaning quiet and compliant. My mom was always telling us kids to not rock the boat or make a scene. Whenever we would express a passionate opinion about something, my mom would give us a disapproving look as if we had done something wrong. My dad, though, gave us more leeway with our opinions and encouraged more independent thinking. I believe he understood the price he had paid in his own life in not living out his dreams, and he didn't want us kids to suffer in the same way. My mom, on the other hand, was entrenched in a victim mentality and unintentionally passed that helplessness and hopelessness onto her kids. Dad's constant message was, "Be true to yourself. Live to your potential." My mother, however, was sending a much different message: "I had to settle in life and so will you. Be happy with whatever life hands you. Suffer in silence."

Taking on both dynamics created an interesting tension within me. Internally, I still possessed a passion and fire for life. I had a wild imagination rivaling that of Walter Mitty. Externally, though, I masked over all of it and revealed it only when I felt safe to do so. I lived vicariously through books and movies but the reality of every day was spent simply trying to stay in others' good graces and avoid conflict. Eventually, I would grow up to be the good employee and the good wife, but I'd pay a high price for it. My dreams had died. My passion had been snuffed out. The very essence of who God made me to be had been sacrificed. I had stopped living and started to simply exist.

But oh, how I wanted to love and be loved! I wanted to experience the full measure of life, to feel deeply, and to express myself passionately. I didn't want to be limited by what others thought or by what society said. I longed to be free—to be who I really was—but the self-imposed prison cell I'd entered back in fifth grade had become pretty comfortable. My interior self clamored to get out but my exterior self held on tightly to the cell keys, certain that being locked up was the safer alternative.

After the end of my first marriage, online dating became an unexpected solution to my dilemma. In the privacy of my home and within the confines of chat rooms, I experienced a measure of freedom without losing control. In reality, I had simply left the jail cell for the prison exercise yard. It was an illusion but it felt like freedom. In chat rooms, I freely expressed myself and gave voice to my passions. Externally, nothing had changed, but internally I felt like a kid in a candy shop. I became even more chameleon-like and the disconnect between who I was in the world and who I was online became even greater.

Chapter 3

UNTIL DEATH DO US PART, TAKE 1

R ememember those "Least Likely" and "Most Likely" titles given in high school yearbooks? If I'd had to title myself, it would have been "Least likely to ever get married." I'd been on only two dates during high school; the first was as a sophomore and my date was a freshman. His brother was dating one of my friends and they decided we might like each other. We chatted a few times on campus and later there was talk of the four of us going on a double date to the movies. About a week before the big date, "Patrick" called and asked me if I'd "go (steady) with him." For some reason, it was important that we have that status before we actually went out on a date. I felt a little weird about it but said yes. For the remainder of that week at school, whenever we were together he would hold my hand. Apparently, that was part and parcel of the going steady agreement. It still felt weird for me since we really didn't know one another and we really weren't what I would consider friends. It was clumsy and awkward and we never said much to one another. Despite all that, it was exciting and flattering to have been noticed and liked. He was a nice looking kid, taller than me with an athletic build, curly blond hair and a ruddy complexion. Our date, though, was weird and that's when I decided that one week of going steady had been enough. We went to see "Phantasm," which wasn't exactly what I would classify as a good date movie unless you (as the guy) wanted your date clinging to your arm the whole time. However, that wasn't the weird part. The thing that sent me packing was the fact that Patrick just stared at me the whole time. I was watching the movie but in my peripheral vision I could see him watching me. Whenever I would turn to look at him, he would smile at me but he never said anything. He just stared at me. It was creepier than the movie. I ended up calling him the following week to break up, though quite frankly, there wasn't much to break up from.

My second high school date was almost as disastrous. I'd gotten to know some kids on campus who turned out to be Christians and we quickly became casual friends. We were nearing the time of our Junior Prom and mutual friends paired me up with "Tad". This time around, things were less date-like since we were attending the prom as part of a group and the pairing up was more of a convenience than a romantic hook-up. However, since the rest of the couples in the group were all dating, there remained an underlying expectation that we might hit it off and become a couple as well. Unfortunately, the two of us didn't have much in common and we were both very shy and quiet. At the prom, the other couples hit the dance floor, leaving me and my date sitting at the table alone. The silence was awkward and I can only imagine how painfully uncomfortable we both must have looked sitting there. I can remember wondering why I'd even bothered. It's not that he wasn't a nice guy—he was polite and gentlemanly and I remember him being soft-spoken, kind of like a young Bob Ross, complete with the sandy brown afro—we just weren't a good fit together and I don't recall spending any time with him after the prom.

After graduating in 1982, my dating life didn't improve much; then again, dance clubs and bars aren't exactly the best places to meet someone of substance. I was still hanging out with a few friends from high school, along with some new friends from work, and we would spend two or three nights each week barhopping and clubbing until the wee hours of the morning. Now, I was only 19 at the time. I shouldn't have been able to get in to any of these places, but when you're young and resourceful you figure out ways to work the system. One bar in particular, located downstairs from its sister restaurant, proved especially susceptible. My friends and I figured out that if we arrived during the dinner hour, there was no one checking ID's at the stairwell leading to the club downstairs. The staff in the club downstairs assumed that someone had already checked our ID's upstairs in the restaurant. Needless to say, we spent a lot of time at that dance club. It was there that I accepted a slow dance invitation one night from a guy who proceeded to nibble my neck and ear and then press himself into me so I could feel what was happening between his legs. Even outside of high school the guys were still creepy, it seemed.

Then there was "Carl". We worked together in the same office and while I had noticed him, he hadn't given me as much as a passing glance—until I lost about 50 pounds. Suddenly he started saying hello, asking how I was, and paying me compliments on my weight loss. That should have been my first indication that he wasn't a man of high character, but I was so flattered by the attention that I overlooked it. I'd never been that thin before and I loved being noticed and admired, even if it was simply for how I looked.

A group of us from work went out that year for St. Patrick's Day. Eventually, Carl and I found ourselves together but not quite alone. We were away from the heavy partying but still in the large hotel courtyard where the festivities were happening. And that's when he kissed me. Despite the raucous environment, it felt like it was just the two of us. A first kiss has the power to transport you like that. It was soft and tender, the way a girl's first kiss should be, and I felt like a princess. There had been no talk of going steady, no friends setting us up, and no dates prior to this one. It was just a random, unexpected moment. I was too young and naïve to realize that it was nothing more than an alcohol-induced impulse on Carl's part. He'd been intrigued by the newly slender girl at the office and had taken advantage of the opportunity when it presented itself. I, on the other hand, was completely smitten. I didn't know anything and I assumed that a kiss meant more than casual interest. For the next couple of weeks, I walked around the office all doe-eyed and giggly, waiting for Carl to sweep me off my feet. He played along for a while but soon got tired of the game and moved on.

As the reality of what happened set in, disappointment and disillusionment claimed their first pieces of my heart. I was hurt and embarrassed. I was ashamed by how I'd behaved in the office, feeling like everyone there had been laughing at me behind my back because they knew the truth. *Silly girl,* I imagined them saying, *she thought he really liked her.* I felt foolish and angry for having let myself entertain such an idea. I decided I wouldn't be so stupid in the future and would take steps to ensure I wasn't hurt like that again. In the midst of that rejection and bitterness, the enemy began to whisper lies: "Men are only interested in your body and that's the only real value you have.", "You're not worthy of a real dating relationship.", "The men you're interested in won't be genuinely interested in you.", "You'll have to settle when it comes to dating.", "Men will just use you and can't be trusted." Sadly, I bought into every one of those statements.

My friends and I continued to visit bars and clubs where my behavior became bolder and more brazen. In contrast to my experience with the slow dancer earlier, I later let a guy paw and manhandle me while talking to him at a club one night, though "let" is an understatement. My body language invited him to kiss me the way the slow dancer had and I took the initiative to press my own body into his. Standing at the bar, we were easily viewed by others in the area. It was an absolute power trip for me and would become a recurring theme in my addiction. Feeling invisible and rejected in my exterior life would drive me to engage in wildly inappropriate behaviors with men later in life as I looked for ways to be seen, noticed, and accepted.

I wasn't looking for a husband but that's exactly who I found when I went to work for a small jewelry store as their credit department manager in the fall of 1984. My experience with Carl earlier that year had soured me on men, so when the women I worked with started telling me that a young waiter from the Farrell's Ice Cream Parlour next door had designs on me, I just blew them off.

We used to order from Farrell's on a regular basis because it was close and convenient; we could call in an order then run next door to pick it up. Pretty soon, though, their waiters started delivering our orders. Not long after, it was just this one waiter in particular.

There was nothing out of the ordinary about the guy, in terms of his looks, but he was outgoing and seemed to have a fun sense of humor. Contrary to what my coworkers thought, I still didn't see any behavior that indicated he was especially interested in me, but that Christmas Eve I was proved wrong. Shortly before closing time, one of the waiters made a special delivery: a stuffed bear with a single long-stemmed red rose and a Christmas card. For me. From that guy.

Wow, I thought, *I guess he was interested.* It was one of the few times I'd been genuinely surprised in my life. While I wasn't especially attracted to the guy, I was flattered by the attention and the effort he had made with the gift and the card. It was the first formal overture anyone had made and that somehow seemed to give him credibility compared to my other experiences. His gesture seemed to melt away a part of the hardness that had begun to creep in after what happened with Carl and I thought that perhaps this guy might be ok.

I quickly ran next door to say thank you and we made plans for a first date on New Year's Day. A week later, Don and I met up with some of his friends and spent the day together. We spent the next day together, too. In fact, we were together every day from our first date until that morning in 1997 when our marriage ended.

About a month into dating, we started discussing marriage. Don proposed to me on Valentine's Day, though as proposals go, it wasn't much to write home about. Because I worked at a jewelry store, I was able to get a discount on the diamond solitaire. I also arranged to have my own ring made and set. Consequently, the proposal wasn't much of a surprise and the delivery method left a little something to be desired. We had been making out in my car when I felt him slip the ring box into my hand. There was no popping of a question, no getting down on one knee, and no romantic setting—just a box and an assumption.

We set a date for October of that year and began making plans. I still remember our meeting with both sets of parents. All of them expressed reservations about the speed of our engagement but, at 20 and 23, we were determined to stick to our timeline because, by golly, we were adults and we knew what we were doing. Of course, we had no idea what we were getting into but no one could tell us anything at that age.

Don and I split our time together between his room at his parents' house, my room at the house I was sharing with roommates, and going out with friends. I don't recall us talking about our lives or making an effort to grow a friendship. Looking back, all we ever really did was make out so it shouldn't have come as much of a surprise when Don started pressuring me to go all the way with him. I was still a virgin at 20 and pretty proud of that fact. It was important to me to wait until marriage and I spent quite a bit of time explaining myself to him. We were only a few months away from the wedding and it didn't seem like a big deal to wait. In hindsight, it seems odd that I was able to say no and not feel like I was missing out on anything despite all the making out we did. I was aroused when we made out but not to the point of feeling out of control. I didn't fully know what I was missing and I think that was a protective measure from God that helped me say no.

With each passing week, Don grew a little more frustrated with me and my refusal to cave in to his requests. It bothered me that he wasn't respecting my decision but not enough to break off the engagement. One day, while making out in my bedroom, partly out of curiosity and partly out of being tired of fighting him on the topic, I relented. Even all these years later, if I close my eyes and concentrate, I can still remember exactly how it felt and what I was thinking. The sex wasn't wild or passionate; it was just kind of matter of fact and then it was over. Don's face had this goofy, euphoric glow. He looked so happy, and I... well, I was just kind of empty. I laid there thinking, *Really? This is why everyone is so on fire to get into someone else's pants? I don't get it. I don't understand the big deal.* Truth be told, I had enjoyed the making out far more than the sex. The act itself was kind of a letdown compared to everything that had led up to it.

Considering my behavior after things with Carl went south, one might think I would have been raring to go with Don, but there's a huge difference between flirtation and follow through and making out and going all the way. My bar behavior after Carl had more to do with control and power and very little to do with sex. It was a way of re-establishing self-worth and a sense of identity by obtaining a man's attention and affection.

With Don, I understood the importance of sex and believed it should have been saved for marriage. I held an almost sacred attitude about it. I knew it was special and I didn't want to cheapen it by engaging in it prematurely, so when we did, I felt disappointed. I wasn't ashamed or embarrassed; I was just sad. It was just one more thing, like the proposal, that hadn't been anything like I'd imagined it would be when I got married.

After that, wedding plans progressed pretty quickly; the closer we got to the date, the faster the time seemed to go. In the last two months before the wedding, I began to sense this little voice telling me to postpone things. I didn't tell anyone because I figured it was just cold feet but the nagging didn't go away. I just had this uneasy feeling a lot of the time. Since Don and I were living together by this time, I simply let the momentum of everything carry me through to the wedding day. We had a civil ceremony in the clubhouse of the apartment complex where we lived and then took a bus ride to Reno for our honeymoon. That was another disappointing experience as we didn't even get to sit together on the ride up there.

Less than one month after the wedding, Don was laid off from Farrell's and later got a job as manager for the Wendy's Hamburgers just down the street from where we lived. That job would end up keeping us apart for the next five years. I worked full-time during the day and he worked full-time mostly at night. We hardly saw one another during that time. We were living under the same roof but we weren't making a life together. The evenings he worked, I visited with either my family or his. I learned to entertain myself and grew a bit of an independent streak during those years, so it wasn't an easy transition when, five years later, he left Wendy's and got a day job at a cardboard manufacturing plant.

All of a sudden, he was underfoot all the time and seemingly always in my way. I'd been married for over five years, but I wasn't used to having a husband.

Chapter 4
THE BEGINNING OF THE END

Familiarity breeds contempt. –**Aesop**

Five years into a marriage isn't the ideal time to discover whom you've married. It's far easier to love someone you barely know when they're hardly around; actually living with them, day in and day out, is a whole 'nother ball of wax.

My husband was a smoker, and having him around at the same time as me made his habit all the more annoying, especially since his housekeeping and hygiene habits left a lot to be desired. Smoking is a dirty habit even under the best of circumstances, but when the smoker isn't neat and tidy it's just plain disgusting. When we were dating, Don had been diligent about keeping his breath fresh, but after five years of marriage he'd stopped caring. Not just about that, but about other aspects of his appearance as well. Understandably, I was no longer interested in kissing or sleeping with an ashtray.

Our sex life, which had improved over time after my first lackluster experience, had deteriorated into a chore for me. Don was interested in things that I wasn't and what should have been a time of intimacy and togetherness usually just ended up as a tense negotiation. Early on in our marriage, we had introduced pornography into the mix. We would rent movies—back in the day when video rental stores actually had an Adult section—as a way of keeping things interesting in the bedroom. Unfortunately, all it did was set us up for failure; it created unrealistic expectations and generated performance anxiety. It also became a crutch. That which you initially bring into your relationship to enhance intimacy becomes the very thing which inhibits it because you can no longer achieve that intimacy without the crutch. Over time, both frequency and satisfaction took a nosedive and we were left to deal with the marriage we had outside of the bedroom. The problem was, outside of the bedroom we didn't have much of a marriage.

Finances were also a constant source of stress and tension in our marriage. My husband had put me in charge of the books, primarily because he had never really taken charge of things when he lived at home. His mom had always prepared his taxes and helped him with other financial matters. When we got married, I took over that role. Every payday, I would check in with him and ask if there was anything he needed. Most of the time he said nothing, but then he would bring up something later in the pay period, like a pair of jeans or some other item. When I told him that there wasn't money in the account for that, he would get upset and complain that there was never any money for the things he wanted. I can't tell you how many times we had this type of conversation. I used to tell him, "I'm not a mind reader. You have to tell me what you need when I ask on payday." He was also absent when it came to other forms of decision making. It was commonplace for Don to defer to my decision, only to come along after the fact and criticize it.

Then came the big reveal. He brought up the one topic that I thought had been clearly settled when we were dating. After about 10 years of marriage, Don told me that he just couldn't imagine the rest of his life without children. Now, we had discussed this topic at length before we got married and I was very clear about my opinion. I told Don, "If there is any chance you're going to want kids, I'm not the girl for you." He replied, "You're all I'll ever need." That rolls off the tongue easily enough when things are going well, but stress the relationship a bit and pretty soon your spouse isn't cutting it for even your most basic needs and desires.

I told Don I would consider adoption. He wasn't opposed to the idea, but he was adamant about us having a child of our own first. I was dead set against getting pregnant and neither of us was willing to budge in the matter. On top of all the other stressors in our marriage, this one topic drove the final nail into the coffin. Just one year later, I came home and discovered his online affair.

My husband moved out of the house that day I learned about Ms. North Carolina. We spent the next few months trying to talk things through and figure out what to do, but he was unwilling to try marriage counseling. He said it hadn't worked for anyone he knew and he didn't believe it would work for us. While Don wasn't doing anything to help our marriage, he also wasn't doing anything to end it. He just wanted to hang out in limbo, keeping me on one side of the fence while he pursued his new interest in North Carolina on the other. That didn't work for me so I decided for him. I told Don he needed to go to North Carolina for a visit. I even helped him make the airline arrangements. My intuition told me they would end up in bed together and I knew that the trip meant the end of our marriage. For some weird reason, though, Don didn't seem to know that. He still seemed to think that he might be able to come back to me and work things out—without the counseling, of course.

When he got back into town, my first question to him was, "Did you sleep with her?" After the briefest hesitation, he admitted they had been intimate. I told him I was filing for divorce. This news, again for some strange reason, seemed to anger him. I just didn't get it. Don had committed adultery and wasn't willing to work on our marriage, yet I was the bad guy. He was treating me like I had done something wrong even though it was Don who had broken the faith between us. It was an eerie foreshadowing of how things would play out in my third marriage.

Shortly thereafter, Don moved to North Carolina. It took six months, but he finally realized that the woman he'd met was simply looking for a meal ticket; she had three small children and was unwilling to get a job. He had been literally killing himself to support them. I found out later, after he came back to town, that Don had been suffering from severe hypertension back east. It was so bad that his doctor administered medication during one visit then forced him to stay in the waiting room to make sure he didn't have a stroke on the drive home.

Six months apart had done a lot to cool our jets. Things had been very contentious when he left and we'd had no contact during most of his absence. I had filed for the divorce and it was about to be finalized when I got a phone call from my soon-to-be ex-mother-in-law. She explained my husband's health issues and asked if I would consider postponing the divorce so that he could get medical coverage under my insurance. At the time, I had the better job working as a state employee and Don had been covered for several years under my medical plan. I wasn't dating anyone at the time, and I didn't have it in me to be vindictive, so I agreed. Whether out of gratitude or some other reason, he called me in response to that news to thank me and to tell me he was returning to town. The conversation was friendly and we made plans to visit.

About a week later, he came by the house. We spent several hours together catching up on things; it was the first pleasant conversation we'd had in a long time. For me, it felt like getting a do-over to be friends in the aftermath of a messy break-up. I figured the time apart had given us both a fresh perspective and had matured us a bit. Over the next few weeks we met for dinner, went to the movies, and took in a baseball game. I even invited him back into my bed. Eventually, Don asked me where "all this" was going. "All what?" I asked. "You know," he replied, "all *this*." Suddenly, I realized what he meant—he thought that "all this" meant we were heading towards reconciliation.

I promptly informed him otherwise. "Why," I asked, "would we get back together when we were so bad at being married?" I was treating him far better as a friend. Why would he want to go back to what we had as husband and wife? Instantly, we stepped six months back in time. "Well," he huffed, "you just don't understand what I've gone through." *Really*, I thought, *silly me for not realizing that you're the only one who's been hurt. You're the only one whose heart has been broken. You're the only one who's suffered in all of this.* I couldn't believe my ears. After all that time, he still didn't get it. He still hadn't apologized for the infidelity. He still hadn't acknowledged how he'd broken the trust and devastated me. There was no repentance for what he'd done; he was just upset that he was suffering the consequences of his actions. He honestly believed that since I'd had six months to sow my own wild oats that I'd be willing to take him back and just pick up where we'd left off.

Well, I'd sown some oats, alright, but I wasn't willing to step back into marriage with him. It had been a mistake to invite him back into my bed—and I'm sure that contributed to him thinking I wanted to reconcile—but reconciliation wasn't what I had in mind when I did it. I'd spent our six months apart cruising through AOL chat rooms flirting and chatting with men from all around the country and after months of having my head filled with all kinds of perverted ideas, I figured I could safely experiment with my husband. But it was awkward, for obvious reasons. He knew the ideas hadn't been mine, and my requests hadn't been made from a place of love. I had merely been satisfying a curiosity and I had used him to do it.

Our divorce was finalized in 1999 and Don remarried about a year after that. He finally got his wish to be a dad; the woman he married had three children, mostly grown at that point, but he still got to parent them for a time. Sadly, after nearly a year of marriage, his hypertension got the best of him. One afternoon while taking a nap, he suffered a heart seizure. Paramedics rushed him to the hospital but it was too late. They told Don's family that even if they'd been right there when it had happened, the seizure was so severe that it wouldn't have mattered.

He was pronounced dead at the hospital at the far too young age of 39.

Looking back at the end of my first marriage, it's interesting to me that I didn't pursue counseling on my own. After all, I had suggested it for the two of us the day I discovered Don's infidelity. For some reason, though, it didn't occur to me to get myself into a good counseling program to deal with the adultery and the divorce. I wish I had; it would have saved me years of damage.

Instead of counseling, I chose to just plow forward into the next season of life carrying 11 years' worth of baggage. That's the problem with not dealing with our past—it will eventually catch up and deal with us. We accumulate junk along the way in life, and if we don't stop to unpack and repack periodically, our load gets heavy and cumbersome. When my marriage ended at the age of 32, I already had quite a load. I not only had marriage issues, I also had childhood issues. I thought I could move on in an "out of sight, out of mind" kind of way. The marriage was over and my husband had passed away. I foolishly believed that meant that all my baggage was gone. However, as

Confucius said, "Wherever you go, there you — and all of your baggage — are."

You can run, but you can't hide from your past. It will follow you around until you face it and deal with it. It will haunt you. It will pester you. It will occasionally rise up and smack you across the face. It will trip you up. It will cause you to stumble. It has the power to imprison you. It is a force to be reckoned with. Make no mistake, your past cannot be ignored but it doesn't have to become a ball and chain that you drag around the rest of your life. Through counseling, you can use your past as a doorway to a new life.

Your past contains a wealth of information — clues about why you do the things you do and keys to new doors in life. There are untold treasures buried in your past, but you have to dig to find them. You won't get much if you just scratch at the surface of things and kick up a little dust. You have to get your hands dirty and you have to dig deep. It takes time and effort. It's a process.

I was never much into processes or taking my time. In school, I hated math. I hated it partly because I never understood it, but I also hated it because the teachers always wanted you to show your work. It wasn't enough to simply answer the questions. You had to write out the process you went through to get the answer; I never understood the value in that. You're asking me a question and I'm giving you an answer. Isn't that good enough?

Part of the reason I hated showing my work is that it didn't allow for wild guesses. You couldn't fake your way through the exam if you had to show your work. You had to know the material in order to prove you knew the material. I just wanted to cruise through the test and move on to the next topic. Learned it. Got it. What's next? That was my attitude in school and it became my attitude in life.

I became an expert at rushing through things super-ficially without evaluating them. My family never dug very deeply into things and I didn't see a need to do it either. Skimming the surface was good enough to get me by. I certainly hadn't taken my time getting to know Don. We had a very shallow friendship and that friendship had never been tested to see if it was strong enough to become a marriage. It's amazing to me that our marriage lasted as long as it did; I believe that rarely seeing one another during those first five years was the only reason we lasted so long.

Once my marriage to Don was over, I figured I had the lessons down pat and could just move ahead in life without analyzing what had happened. Besides, I felt like I had done that. I had discussed the end of the marriage at great length with my ex-mother-in-law, my friends, and my coworkers. We had come up with our theories and explanations, boxed them all up, and tied them all together with a big red bow. What more was needed?

After discovering my husband's adultery, I spent months diving into the world of AOL chat rooms. An increasingly interesting distraction, it was definitely more pleasant than digging through my past and revisiting all that rejection and betrayal. I didn't want to get healthy; I just wanted to feel good. Even more than that, I wanted to try out my newly single legs. Don was only the third person I'd dated and I knew there were a lot more fish in the sea. I'd settled in my first marriage and I didn't plan on making that mistake again. As I would later tell friends, "There was a smorgasbord of men out in the world and I was a starving woman."

Chapter 5

FREE, WHITE, AND WELL OVER 21

I felt like I was going to throw up. I had just parked my car in the underground structure in Old Sacramento and was about to head upstairs to meet him for the first time. I don't recall the circumstances of our online chats but I clearly remember our first and only date. After months of chatting and flirting with strangers online, this was my first face-to-face meeting with someone from the internet, and I was sick to my stomach.

I sat in my car trying to calm down. *Breathe deeply,* I thought. *In through the nose, out through the mouth.* But the more I tried to slow my breathing, the more I could hear my heart hammering away in my ears. *This isn't working. Maybe I should just start the car and drive back home.* After all, he'd never seen me and I could just block him in the chat rooms. No harm, no foul. *You're going to have to do this eventually*, I told myself. *There has to be a "first" first date at some point. May as well be today.*

I got out of my car, still feeling queasy. Standing up was a little better but not much. I started walking and hoped my legs would hold. They felt wobbly and shaky, almost like I was trying them out for the first time. I stepped carefully, deliberately, still trying to work on my breathing. Slowly, I made my way to the place where we had decided to meet and waited. That, in itself, was awkward and would always remain the most uncomfortable part about online dating. It's one thing to arrive at a meeting place and wait for someone you know; it's entirely another to arrive and look like you're waiting for someone you've only ever seen in a photo. I felt like there was a marquee running across my forehead telling the world, *"I'm waiting for a date. I've never seen him before. I met him online because I'm not capable of meeting a date in a normal way."* At the time, online dating was in its infancy and it had a bit of a stigma attached to it. It wasn't nearly as pervasive as it is today. Nowadays, you can't go more than one commercial break without seeing an ad for some kind of online dating service on television or hearing one on the radio—it's absolutely a given on the internet. Pop-up ads are everywhere and there's a dating site for every life circumstance and culture. But back on that day in Old Sacramento, it definitely wasn't the norm.

My date eventually showed up and we spent a couple of hours walking around and talking. I can't tell you his name or what he looked like, but I do remember that we got ice cream at one point and I remember the dress I was wearing. More than that, I remember the feeling of relief when I got back to my car. "First date under the belt," I whispered to myself. "You can do this. You can get back out into the dating scene." My husband had been only my third date in life, and I'd been unavailable for over 11 years, so "getting back into" dating was really an overstatement. I was actually just entering the dating world for the first time at the age of 33.

I mistakenly believed that because I had been married for so long that I knew and understood men. Sharing my marriage experience with others online lulled me into a false reality. I began to believe I had a better handle on who I was than I really did. That's one of the problems with online addiction; you begin to buy into your own hype. You start to believe the things you tell others and you begin to act on what you think is true about yourself. Pretty soon, you're living out the lies, both those that you believe and those that you tell.

I titled this chapter with a quote I often used when talking about my online dating life, especially when it came to dating married men. In my brokenness, I didn't see a problem with being the other woman. I figured that the problem was in the guy's marriage because he was the one who had made a commitment. On the other hand, I was single and could do whatever I wanted. You would think that I would have been vehemently opposed to contributing to infidelity in someone else's marriage precisely because of what had happened in my own — and that might have been the case had I received counseling and actually dealt with my divorce. Unfortunately, I simply boomeranged to the other end of the spectrum and threw responsibility and caution to the wind. I was free to do whatever, with whomever, and whenever I wanted. I didn't concern myself with who might get hurt in the process, which leads me to a man I'll call "Stuart".

He was the first married man I met, and he was the first man I was physically intimate with after my divorce. We met in a chat room one night and started discussing baseball, of all things. We continued visiting the same chat room night after night and it wasn't long before we were logging in to chat exclusively with each other. Stuart was intelligent and had a sharp wit, and we would spend hours discussing a variety of topics. It's important to note here that people who hang out online are not stupid, nor are they all computer nerds. We can be accused of a lot of things — being broken, lonely, addicted, and even temporarily insane — but stupid we are not. There are a lot of intelligent and interesting people who hold high-paying, responsible jobs who spend their time in chat rooms. Addiction and adultery are not the bane of any one particular people group; we are all susceptible.

After chatting online for a couple of months, Stuart asked if I'd like to meet. We were both going to be in the Los Angeles area for work and decided to make plans. There are a number of men that I met and slept with during my years of addiction whose names I don't remember, and I can barely recall the circumstances surrounding our time together, but I remember everything about Stuart. Firsts are like that, even in addiction. I remember that he mailed me a couple of CDs so that we could listen to the same music while we chatted online; I even remember the artists and specific songs that were favorites. I recall that he wore a green blazer the night we met in the lobby bar at the Biltmore in downtown L.A., and I can still remember the drive to Peppone's in the convertible he'd rented.

There had been an amazing sunset that night and we got to enjoy it nearly the entire drive to Brentwood.

Everything about our dinner that night is still clear as a bell: the bar where we waited for our table, the booth where we sat, the dish Stuart got me to try by telling me the calamari was really a piece of pasta, the waiter who sounded like he'd just gotten off the boat from Italy, and the amazing desserts we tried. The entire restaurant experience could be described in one word — *decadent.*

When we returned to the Biltmore, we ordered a couple of drinks and curled up on one of the lobby sofas to chat for a while. I was absolutely over the moon for that time we spent together. For the first time in my life, I felt truly desired. More than that, I felt desirable. Stuart had treated me like a queen that night and made me feel special; that was the high for me. It didn't matter that he wasn't available for a relationship. All I cared about was feeling good.

We eventually made our way back to Stuart's room for the real reason we'd met. Again, I remember minute details — the plantation shutters on the windows, the layout of the room, and talking about how he wore Escada cologne — but I remember other things, too. I remember the panic that set in after we'd been intimate and how I couldn't wait to get back to my own room. I'm certain Stuart assumed that I would spend the night with him, but all of a sudden I needed to be by myself, and not just for the night. I got back to my room and immediately began thinking about how I could break things off with Stuart. A few days later, I emailed him and told him that I just wanted to be friends. He replied, and I'm quoting, "I won't be your dick in a jar."

My experience with Stuart began to cement the lies that men and women could only relate to one another through sex and that men would find me interesting only if sex was involved. This experience also set the pattern in terms of my preferred type of man. I would usually gravitate towards older men — usually at least ten years older than me, in professional occupations — who were generous with their time and wallets. "Joe" was one such man.

I met Joe one night after a few hours of chatting online. As was common with the married men I met, he didn't send me a photo. Instead, he just described himself in response to my photo. After all, who wants to be seen and known when you're planning to commit adultery? We met at a Denny's, and after a couple of hours there, made plans to drive to Lake Tahoe later that same day. We never made it to Tahoe but we did spend the remainder of his business trip together. That was the beginning of a longer-term affair spanning numerous months and ending with Joe flying me down to San Diego for a long weekend while he was there on business. It's pretty heady stuff, being someone's mistress. I remember the two of us getting to the hotel in San Diego and Joe giving me cash for the bellman's tip, along with his room key, then giving me a kiss and sending me upstairs with the luggage while he picked up some things in the business center. It was one of those weird moments that looks and feels like trust and intimacy, and makes you feel like a couple, but it's really just an illusion. It's those types of moments which often lead a woman to believe the man will eventually leave his wife for her. I, on the other hand, had no such illusions. Even in my addiction, I knew enough to know that the married men I dated were never going to leave their families for me. I understood the rules of the game and I always played by them.

Besides, I was in it for the high—for the experience of being spoiled. I desperately wanted attention and affection, and married men were only too willing to oblige. In return, they got what they desperately needed: *respect*. The married men I dated got their egos boosted and their pride stroked. They felt important and interesting in the eyes of a woman, and if you've ever doubted how necessary that is for a man, let me tell you that they are willing to pay a high price for it. Those men risked their marriages for it and spent cold, hard cash to spoil me during our time together. Even Stuart had offered at one point to fly me all over the west coast and join him on business trips, an offer I had refused at the time.

During some of my most broken thinking, I would begin evaluating the merit of remaining single but dating only married men, essentially prostituting myself. For a brief time, I would actually believe that was a good plan for my life, but it was just a broken and twisted take on meeting the love and respect needs that the Bible outlines. God wired women to be loved and He wired men to be respected.[5] God calls each of us to be sacrificially loving and respectful to each other even – dare I say, especially – when they haven't earned it. God first modeled that sacrificial behavior when He went to the cross and died for each one of us and He calls us to do the same. I, and the married men I dated, were sacrificing but not in the ways God intended. I sacrificed my self-respect in order to gain love, and the men I dated sacrificed the love they may have been getting at home in order to gain respect.

We were missing the mark in terms of what we were sacrificing and why we were sacrificing it. God calls us to crucify and sacrifice the things of our flesh — things like pride, ego, selfishness, and self-righteousness — but He doesn't call us to sacrifice those things in order to gain something. The Bible says that those who have been forgiven much, love much.[6] Jesus forgave the insurmountable debt of sin in our life, giving His own life as payment for it. Through His sacrifice we have been given the great gift of eternal life. Out of gratitude for that gift, we overflow with love towards God and others and from that heart of love we sacrifice, not for our gain but for the benefit of others.

Erotica is defined as literature or art designed to arouse sexual desire; it's a nice little euphemism to make it more palatable, as if it's refined or artsy. But let's be clear about something: it's pornography, plain and simple, and I spent a lot of time writing and sharing it during the years after my divorce.

Did you know that if you're not using your God-given gifts in the ways He intended, the enemy will come along and pervert them? Writing has always come easily to me, even as a child. It's been a gift of God from the beginning, but in the absence of a relationship with Christ, I ended up using that gift as a means to enslave others and draw them deeper into their own sexual addictions and perversions. The enemy hijacked God's gifting within me and leveraged it for his own purposes—to steal, kill and destroy.[7]

Even after all this time, these are not easy words to type. As I started to write these chapters detailing my addiction, I asked God to bring to my mind the things He wanted me to share. In the process, I've remembered things long forgotten. One such memory involved all of the erotic artwork that I had saved on my computer at the time. I had numerous websites bookmarked for artists specializing in erotic photography. Back then, I considered it art and it wasn't uncommon for me and those I chatted with to share pictures and talk about them. From there, it wasn't much of a leap to begin viewing video clips and sharing those, as well. Couples loved to film themselves and then post the videos on various websites. Sometimes, the people I chatted with had videos of their own that they would send me. It was always meant as a way to gauge your tolerance and interest in all things sexual. Would you be willing to engage in a threesome? Bondage? Dominant/submissive scenarios? Did you have a thing for being watched by others, or watching others? Were you into using toys and other paraphernalia? The list goes on and on.

In the chat rooms, if you were curious, you could join the discussion and ask questions. Or you could simply lurk, collecting information silently as you watched the discussion scroll across your computer screen. Those rooms, and the ensuing private chats, were the perfect opportunity for me to share my writing. It started simply enough, often as a tandem writing exercise between me and another person. One of us would make a comment about what we might do to the other and the other person picked up the scenario and added their comments to it. Those rooms were my training ground and it wasn't long before I started writing out both sides of the conversation on my own, crafting short stories.

Writing erotica gave me an advantage over most of the other people in the chat rooms I visited. All I had to do was toss out that piece of information as bait and pretty soon I had private message boxes appearing all over my screen with requests to read my stories. At the time, I believed that writing erotica was the most interesting thing about me. It's not that I didn't have other interests, because I did, but writing erotic stories was the one thing that generated the most interest from others, and I was all about making connections with the hope of meeting in person.

One of the primary complaints about pornography is that it objectifies women, but we rarely hear about how a woman uses pornography to objectify men or even to objectify herself. That's the category I fell into. I was convinced that my only real value to men was as a source of sexual fulfillment. I didn't believe that a man would be interested in me if sex wasn't somehow involved and I believed that the greatest asset I brought to the relational table was that of my sexual persona. Having friendship rejected by both my first husband and by Stuart contributed greatly to me believing these lies and it began to change how I saw myself over time. I stopped seeing myself as a person of value simply because I existed, and started seeing myself as something that had value only when it was used for its supposed purpose. I used pornography to further define that sexual persona and to further objectify myself. Did the men I slept with use me? Absolutely, but they couldn't have done it had I not seen myself as an object first. That's not to say that there isn't a lot of involuntary objectification going on in the world. I just think it's important to realize that there are also a lot of women in the world participating in consensual sex who have unintentionally objectified themselves and need help to break that cycle of thinking.

Additionally, men usually get labeled as the ones who are into chasing and conquering when it comes to dating, but I was guilty of the same thing. I desired those chat room connections so badly because I was addicted to the attention and the pursuit that would soon follow. If we made plans for a date, it was almost guaranteed to end up in bed, even on a first date. For a time, I even nicknamed myself "Queen of the One-Night Stand." At the time, I would have sworn to you that I desperately wanted to be in a long-term, monogamous relationship but my behavior told a different story. The truth was that I loved the *idea* of a long-term, monogamous relationship, but in reality, I just loved the chase and the conquest. I loved the flirting, the enticing, and the teasing. Getting a man into bed was the epitome of achievement for me back then. I felt powerful and purposeful. Seducing and satisfying a man gave meaning and reason to my life, but it also was a way of maintaining some semblance of control and distance.

Because I'd never dealt with the damage caused by my divorce, there was tremendous fear attached to commitment. It was far safer to just be casual with men and enjoy a false sense of intimacy and closeness.

I desperately wanted to be known and understood, but I also knew that if anyone looked too deeply they would find nothing. I felt empty, and chasing after dates was how I attempted to fill the void. The combination of my dating addiction and sexual sin created a vicious downward spiral. I would chase after relationships in the hope of finding "the one," and I would use sex to prove my worth and value as a partner to them. However, once I'd achieved that intimacy with them, fear of having my emptiness discovered would kick in and I would begin to behave in ways that pushed men away. Rejection and disappointment would result and I'd go off in search of another date, starting the cycle all over again.

Chapter 6
COLLATERAL DAMAGE

ddiction doesn't live in a vacuum. It doesn't just impact and hurt the one who is suffering from the addiction. There is always collateral damage in the lives of those close to the addict.

My closest friend during my early years of promiscuity was a woman I'll call Sue. We'd met and become friends through work and I used to spend quite a bit of time with her and her family. She was married and had two small children at the time. Her husband worked for a local police department and the two of them did a lot of philanthropic work for the community. We had been friends for several years before my addiction started, so there was an established level of trust and transparency between us. There was very little, if anything, that we withheld from one another.

As I started to spend more and more time online, that topic began to dominate my half of the conversation during our visits. Being a good friend, she wanted to know and understand what I was getting myself into. Unfortunately, instead of cautioning me about things, she ended up joining me in my addiction.

Sue had a crafting room at one end of her home and that's where we spent most of our time together; it was private and it had a computer. It wasn't long before we were spending most of our visits online in chat rooms. Sue eventually met a man named "Mark" who worked as a firefighter in Chicago. They hit it off and pretty soon they were chatting regularly even when I wasn't around. One day, Sue announced that she wanted to meet Mark. My first response was "Absolutely not! You're married, and he could be a psycho." Funny how we're so quick to see the problems and risks with other people's behavior and so slow to recognize it in our own life. Had I been more willing to see and remove the plank in my own eye, I might have saved myself and others an awful lot of pain and suffering.

Months went by and my friend was still talking about meeting Mark. She finally told me that she was making definite plans to meet him and she wanted to use me as her alibi by telling her husband we were planning a girls' weekend at the coast. At first, I refused, but the more I thought about it, the more I worried that she was going off to meet some crazy person. I felt stuck between the proverbial rock and hard place. Whether or not I accompanied her, I felt like she was walking into disaster. Finally, after weeks of refusing her request, I relented and agreed to go with her.

When Sue and I finally met Mark, I was prepared to hate him. I knew my friend was beyond excited to meet him but I just saw him as a homewrecker. *With all the single women online*, I thought, *and this guy had to pursue my married friend?* I still couldn't see the similarities between his behavior and mine, and I never did put two and two together. As it turned out, Mark was a nice guy. I didn't want to like him but I did. He was courteous to us both and he had a quiet, humble way about him. I'm not sure what I expected, but it wasn't that. After we all had dinner together, Sue left to spend the night with Mark in his room. That was the first of three trips Sue and I took to meet Mark that year. In between all those trips, a mutual friend and I continued to encourage Sue to break things off but she was completely smitten. She even started talking about leaving her husband and going back to Chicago to live with Mark.

Not too long after the last trip, I got a phone call. I answered the phone and immediately recognized the voice — it was Sue's husband. Before I could get anything past "Hello" out of my mouth, he began reading me the riot act. How dare I keep secrets from him and his family? How could I have shared their dinner table, knowing that Sue was having an affair right under his nose? He blamed the affair on me and all my stories about online dating. He ended the call by telling me that I was no longer welcome in their home and that I was to stay away from his wife. I stood there in my kitchen, holding the dead phone line in my hand, wondering what had happened. It had been pretty clear from his comments that Sue had thrown me and our mutual friend under the bus and had somehow implicated us as the primary culprits in the affair. I called our mutual friend, and sure enough, she'd gotten a similar phone call. About a week later, I finally heard from Sue but it was only to tell me she could no longer talk with me. Her husband had instituted martial law in their house. He drove her to work and picked her up. He monitored all of her cell phone calls — she had called me from work — and email. She had become a prisoner in her home and in her marriage.

That was the last I heard from Sue. I don't know if she and her husband ever worked through the affair and healed from it. I don't know if she ended up filing for divorce and leaving him. I don't know if she and Mark ever ended up together. What I do know is that my addiction became her addiction, and her affair devastated their family.

Addiction doesn't live in a vacuum and neither do people. The way we live our life has tremendous impact on those around us. It's a myth that addiction only hurts the addict. Other lives can just as easily be hurt or destroyed and the addict has to live with those consequences. By the grace of God, He has forgiven me for the role I played in Sue's affair, but that forgiveness doesn't erase the memory and it doesn't undo the damage. I wish that life's lessons could be learned more easily, but I've discovered that the greatest lessons are the ones that have come through the greatest pain and suffering. They leave the deepest scars and they are the ones that have the power to most radically transform us, if we let God have them, for it is only through Him that rebellion can become redemption.

My friend, Sue, wasn't the only one to suffer at the hands of my addiction. My family suffered, as well.

The more I chased after dating relationships, the more I ignored my family. It wasn't uncommon for me to blow off plans with my sister or my parents for a date if I landed one. My loyalty was to my addiction; my family was a distant second. Even when I was spending time with them, most of what I talked about was my dating life. It consumed my thoughts and distracted me from really connecting with my family.

Those are years that I'll never get back. When my dad was diagnosed with Alzheimer's, I regretted not having connected more fully with him when his memory was intact. When my sister recently separated from her husband and distanced herself from my mom—following a similar path to mine—I regretted not having been a better example to her. Blinded by our brokenness, we often don't realize the damage we're causing. Sometimes, it's not until years later that we fully realize the consequences of our actions.

However, the person who suffered most because of my addiction was me. I engaged in terribly risky behaviors, sometimes placing myself in dangerous situations. With one individual, I exposed myself to herpes during unprotected sex. On another occasion, I found myself knocking on a date's door at about midnight in midtown Sacramento. Three young men were walking down the opposite side of the street towards me. In a moment of panic, I thought, *I've pushed the boundary one too many times and now it's too late*. I figured they were friends of the guy I was meeting and that I was about to be forcibly taken into his apartment for who knows what. By the grace of God, they weren't and I wasn't, but I never should have been in that part of town at that hour in the first place. On business trips, I invited men I'd only met online up to my hotel room. I got into cars with men I'd only just met online and I invited them to my home. I was reckless and foolish, not just with my body but with my heart.

Proverbs 4:23 cautions us to guard our heart above all else because it is the wellspring of life. Not only was I not guarding my heart, I was exposing it to all kinds of injury. Every time I slept with someone, I was creating a connection to them; that's how God designed sex to work. Our bodies release oxytocin during sex and that hormone is meant to deepen and strengthen feelings of attachment. That's why we feel so close after we've been physically intimate and that's why God created sex as a gift to be enjoyed within marriage only. Outside of marriage, physical intimacy damages our heart. Every sexual encounter fuses our heart with someone else's, and when we move on to someone else there is a separation that occurs between our heart and theirs. The next time we sleep with someone, our heart once again fuses to theirs. We move on and our heart experiences separation once again. Imagine what the heart begins to look like after a number of partners, all mucked up with tattered remnants from those encounters.[8] After a while, you can't see your own heart buried under all that build-up.

I was also damaging my self-esteem. The more I engaged in casual sex, the more I saw myself as a sexual being only, and the more I behaved from that mindset. Between that and never having learned about healthy boundaries, I had no idea who I really was. The person God made me to be was nowhere in sight. Instead, the person I was at that time lived a "less than" life, settling for the scraps that men tossed my way. I was often the fix-it date or the transition girlfriend—the one that men could date and sleep with while they rebounded from someone they really cared about. I'd listen to their problems and would encourage and counsel them. Afterwards, when they felt healthy enough to move on to a real relationship, they were gone.

My reputation in the workplace took a hit during this time as well. Wisdom and discernment weren't strong suits and I often shared details about my dating life that should have remained private. This was in the days before Facebook so my sharing took place around the proverbial water cooler at the office. Sleeping around made me feel important. Because I'd felt so invisible in the world all my life, I shared dating details with coworkers and friends in the hope that they would see me as special and valuable, but that wasn't how they saw me at all. One of my coworkers finally commented that she needed a scorecard to keep up with my dating life because the players were simply changing too fast. That's not admiration; that's a subtle form of condemnation.

Addiction creates a special kind of blindness in our life. We are unable see ourselves or our behavior accurately. Additionally, we lose our ability to evaluate life circumstances properly. That particular blindness was about to lead me into an event that, to this day, I can only explain as temporary insanity.

I met "Kevin" in early 2002. Like everyone else I'd met, Kevin was an online encounter. He was in his late 30's and living in New Jersey. Aside from those two pieces of information, I don't remember much about him, which makes what I did all the more incomprehensible. We had been chatting online and on the phone for a few months when I decided that he was "the one". I was ready to run away and live happily ever after with him, "running away" being the key phrase here. My addiction was all about running away from myself and my past, and never about running towards something or someone. I was always trying to escape my boredom, my loneliness, and my lack of meaning and purpose in life. I was always looking to another person as the source of a new life. It would be another five years before I would encounter God in a significant way and realize that He was the only One who could truly give me a new life.

Kevin and I started making plans for our future together. I decided I would quit my job with the State of California and move to New Jersey. It wouldn't have been quite so crazy if I'd made the decision after a series of successful visits. Instead, I made the decision and resigned from my job *before I'd ever laid eyes on Kevin in person.* My last day at work was the day Kevin arrived in town. Our plan was to spend two weeks at my place, pack up my things, then drive back to New Jersey and start our life together. But just a few days after his arrival, I knew it wasn't going to work. After one week, I bought a plane ticket for Kevin and sent him home to New Jersey, alone. That night, I clearly remember drawing a bath for myself. As I sat there soaking, I suddenly sat upright and thought, *Good Lord, what have I done? I quit my job and I have nothing else lined up!*

It was the first time I'd ever left a job without having another one ready to go, but it wasn't just any job I'd left. I had been working as a conference planner and things had been on the upswing. I had recently been published in an industry trade magazine and had spoken as a panelist at a couple of sales and tourism events. I'd also just been named Meeting Planner of the Year by our local trade organization. I hadn't just walked away from a job; I'd left a career.

Whenever I share this story, I always get asked what my friends thought. Did they caution me against such a wild decision? Did they try to talk me out of it? Did they tell me I should wait? I told anyone who would listen that I was packing up my entire life and moving back east to live happily ever after with someone I'd never met in person. I told my coworkers and I told my friends in the industry. Most of the responses were, "That's so romantic!" or "It's just like in the movies!" Some friends called my decision "wild and crazy" but no one came right out and challenged me to slow down or reconsider. A current friend of mine, when hearing about those responses, said, "I think you needed better friends!" I think he was right.

Honestly, though, even if someone had objected, I still would have plowed ahead. I was convinced I was doing the right thing. It wasn't until Kevin arrived and we started spending time together that I began to sober up and my decision started to sound as crazy as it was. The weekend Kevin arrived, we attended a birthday party for my aunt and it was only there that I received sidelong glances and less than enthusiastic responses to my news. Family members were the only ones who expressed any real concern.

After sending Kevin home, I eventually decided I'd had enough of the government bureaucracy and red tape, and saw my resignation as a chance to start over. I cashed out the few tax-sheltered annuities I had, paid off my bills, and started volunteering at a local hypnotherapy school. A couple of months later, I sold the mobile home I'd been stuck with after the divorce and moved in with the owner of the hypno-therapy school where I'd started to work full-time. My employment arrangement wasn't formal at all. I worked when the owner worked and she simply wrote me a check whenever I needed money — no set paydays or pay rate and no set work schedule. I attended the hypnotherapy class that semester as part of my compensation, along with a few other therapeutic classes. It was a very New Age environment and I bought into all of it: crystals, shakras, tarot cards, palm reading, psychic readings, horoscopes, and past life regression. I was searching desperately for something or someone I could anchor myself to in life. I wanted to be well, even though I had no clue what being well looked like. I just knew it was something other than the life I was living at the time.

When all of those New Age alternatives failed to satisfy, I once again turned to online dating. This time, though, God would harness it to bring me a breath of fresh air and some sanity in the midst of the craziness at the school.

Chapter 7

UNTIL DEATH DO US PART, TAKE 2

John's profile wasn't anything special. I'd been looking at Match.com ads and there were a few that had caught my attention, including his. He wasn't extraordinarily handsome, nor was his profile exceptionally interesting, yet there was something about it. I kept coming back to look at his ad and would just stare at his picture as if I could somehow glean more information from it. *This is ridiculous*, I thought, *just send him an email already.* I sent off a quick note of introduction and waited; his reply arrived later that evening. In it, he addressed me as "Pretty Lady," a pet name that would remain for the rest of our relationship.

We exchanged a few emails, then a few phone calls. We made plans to meet for lunch on March 21, 2003. Going into that first meeting, I was cautiously optimistic. Dates usually fell into one of two categories for me: I was either very physically attracted to them, but bored out of my mind when it came to conversation, or I was fascinated with our conversations but not physically attracted to them at all. I had yet to meet someone whom I found attractive, both physically and mentally. John and I had hit it off in our phone calls and he was easy to talk with. I'd seen his photo in the ad but knew better than to trust it. Outdated photos were commonplace in online dating ads. I was hoping his photo had not done him justice.

I got to the restaurant early and waited in the lobby. Little did I know that John had arrived even earlier and had been waiting in the parking lot. Apparently, I didn't have the corner on the caution market. I'll never forget sitting in that lobby, seeing the door open and laying eyes on John for the first time. My first and only thought was, "Thank you, Jesus, he's good looking, too!" I wasn't close to being a Christ-follower at that time but I was only too happy to thank God in that moment. In his picture, John's hair and goatee had been light brown in color but when he walked in to that restaurant it was obvious he had stopped dying his hair. I couldn't have been happier. Without the dye, his hair and goatee were a beautiful salt and pepper and it gave him a rakish, mischievous look. He bore a strong resemblance to Boz Scaggs and had sometimes been mistaken for him in his younger years.

John was 12 years older than me. He had been married once and divorced, and had served his country honorably during the Vietnam War. The part of me that wanted to be needed was instantly attracted. I saw him as someone who needed care and kindness in his life, and I wanted to be the one to provide those things. I believe that part of my attraction to older men stemmed from the lie that I had to settle in life. I thought older men weren't as choosy and that they would be more willing to engage in relationship with me, grateful for the attentions and affections of a significantly younger woman. I also saw them as more needy and dependent than men closer to my age. On the upside, I loved that they were old-fashioned and gentlemanly. They were far more likely to hold doors open for me, offer me their coat, hold my chair, and generally treat me like a lady ought to be treated.

Lunch was a success and we made plans for a more formal date. Later that week, we met for dinner at a small Italian restaurant close to the school where I was living. In the middle of that dinner, though no one was sitting next to me in the booth, I clearly heard the words, "This is the man you're going to spend the rest of your life with." I knew in that moment that John was a good and decent man and that I was going to commit my heart to him, a feeling that was reinforced during my first visit to his home. John was an amazing cook and he went all out for that visit. He had typed up a menu commemorating our date and there were flowers and a card waiting for me. Cards would become a staple in our relationship and they would grace my cubicle at work in the years to follow. We sat on his deck overlooking a small lake and talked away the entire afternoon while holding hands. It was our third date and John hadn't let things get physically intimate yet. At the time, I didn't realize what a gift that was, but I knew he was different from the other men I'd met. I felt safe and protected in his presence. He wasn't out to use me; he actually wanted to get to know me and be my friend.

Part of that friendship involved telling me the truth about my situation at the hypnotherapy school. John was appalled that I didn't have regular working hours or a set income and pay schedule. "There are labor laws in California," he told me. He encouraged me to have a conversation with the owner of the school, which I eventually did. I asked for regular work hours at the office so that I could plan for time with John. Almost immediately, the owner became passive-aggressive with me and resentment began to build. But while the situation was deteriorating at the school, things were progressing between me and John and we began talking about moving in together. However, we didn't want to take that step out of need. I didn't want to move in with him unless I had a steady job and income and could contribute to the household. I eventually moved out of the school and moved in with my sister and brother-in-law while I looked for a full-time job. A couple of weeks later, I was gainfully employed once again and two weeks after that, I moved in with John.

Dating someone provides only so much information about them. It's not until you live with them full-time that you really begin the journey of discovery. As John and I got to know one another in the three months before moving in together, I learned a few things about his health. I knew he had served in Vietnam and had been exposed to Agent Orange. I knew he had returned home and had been immediately diagnosed with non-Hodgkins lymphoma. He had been treated with experimental doses of radiation which killed the cancer but also started to kill off other vital systems in his body, including his circulation, which had resulted in three open heart surgeries. John also suffered from lymphedema along with neuropathy in both legs and feet. He was very transparent about his health issues and disclosed all of it to me. Nevertheless, it's one thing to be told about health issues like that and quite another to live with them day in and day out.

When we were dating, John always put on a good face but once we were living together I saw who he was after our dates had ended. I saw him in pain 24/7. I learned about all of the prescription medications he was taking. I witnessed his herculean efforts to live a normal life and maintain his home on the lake. And, I watched him bury his pain under alcohol each evening.

Our life together, while filled with a number of social activities, primarily focused on his health and it eventually consumed most of our free time. When we weren't monitoring his medications, we were at the doctor's office. Whenever John developed cellulitis, we packed up and admitted him to the hospital for a few days so they could pump him full of antibiotics. When John's potassium levels got out of whack, either too high or too low, that required admission to the hospital, as well. After we discovered he had lymph-edema, we took classes to learn how to care for that condition at home. Each day, John would put on thigh-high compression stockings and each night I wrapped his legs with gauze, foam padding, and ace bandages to compress them and force the accumulated fluid out of his lower body and into his already compromised lymphatic system. About 18 months into our rela-tionship, John started gaining water weight, a dan-gerous condition for someone with congestive heart failure. We admitted him to the hospital once again but it wasn't days later that he was discharged, it was weeks; six, to be exact. After he was released, he had one more issue added to his health resume': kidney failure. Our health care routine, which had already been quite full, became even more demanding. Three days each week, John visited a dialysis center where he was connected to a machine which acted as an arti-ficial kidney. The process, which usually took about four hours, removed the impurities from his blood and balanced out his electrolyte and mineral levels, a job that his kidneys could no longer perform due to his heart failure.

With all of these health issues, it shouldn't have come as a surprise to me that our sex life would be limited, but it did. John and I were physically intimate on four separate occasions, all occurring in the first 18 months of our relationship. I'd like to tell you that when I realized the extent of the limitation in that area of our life, I was full of understanding and compassion and I accepted the news graciously, but that would be a lie. I pouted and I sulked. I was deeply disappointed and I felt cheated. I was 38 when I met John, and after years of sleeping around with strangers, I was looking forward to having an exclusive partner and engaging in physical intimacy whenever I wanted. I loved John and wanted to enjoy that feeling of being one flesh with him. With all of the medical issues we faced on a daily basis, sex had been one of the few islands of normal and healthy in our relationship; to have even that taken away was devastating for me.

It took the better part of a year for me to grieve the loss of our physical relationship. There was anger, bitterness, resentment, and self-pity that had to be processed. I had to let go of what we couldn't have in order to embrace what we did. Despite the lack of sex, we had a very affectionate relationship. Holding hands was a very big deal for us and we did it everywhere we went. We were almost always touching one another in some fashion: putting an arm around the other or caressing their back, massaging their shoulders or neck, resting a hand on the other's leg, or coming up behind the other and giving them a hug. Last but not least, there were good old-fashioned kisses thrown in for good measure.

The affection went a long way towards easing my disappointment about our non-existent sex life, but the real reason our relationship not only survived but flourished, was due to our friendship. Our love for one another wasn't based on sexual attraction; it was based on things like honesty and trust. We had been through the wringer with John's health and neither one of us had called it quits. He often told me that I should leave him for someone younger and healthier, and I imagine he steeled himself each time to hear that I was taking him up on his offer. But each time I refused and chose to stand by him through yet another challenge, trust was built and our relationship was strengthened and deepened. John knew I was sad about the lack of physical intimacy, but my actions demonstrated to him how important he was to me. I wasn't with him for the sex. I wasn't with him for the money (his medical retirement income was pretty limited). I wasn't with him for his material wealth (his home on the lake was a 32' fifth-wheel trailer). I loved him and I was with him because of who he was. And I didn't just love him; I liked him. I respected him and I trusted him. I was absolutely committed to him. He was my best friend and I was his. We had our petty squabbles like every other couple, but because of our friendship our disagreements didn't last long. We simply couldn't stand to be apart physically or emotionally.

Amid all of the medical appointments, John and I managed to squeeze in some really special moments. In 2004, John and I packed up and headed west to Half Moon Bay for my 40th birthday. We had reservations at a lighthouse-themed hotel right on the beach. I loved lighthouses and I loved the beach, so it was a perfect destination. One of my favorite pictures of John was taken in that hotel room. It's a bittersweet memory, though. Less than a month later, we would admit John to the hospital for a six-week stay that would mark the beginning of the end of his life. That picture, and that trip, represent some of the last healthy moments I got to enjoy with John.

Christmas the year before was also pretty special. It was the kind of Christmas Day I'd always wanted to have, and it's one of my favorite memories of John. We had both gone a little crazy shopping for one another that year, and in a weird coincidence, we had gotten each other the exact same number of gifts. We had stuffed stockings, too. I was more excited for John to empty his because I had purchased his wedding ring and buried it in the toe of his stocking. We had gotten up early that morning and I had put a pan of orange cinnamon rolls in the oven and made coffee. John made a fire and we settled in to open gifts. It was a perfect morning — coffee and pastry, a roaring fire, and the love of my life by my side.

Camping trips also provided some special memories. John loved to camp, but anyone who knows me knows that I'm far less enthusiastic about it — I actually hate it. I told John as much when he first broached the topic. "Thanks, but no thanks," I had told him. He had friends who could join him. He didn't need me to tag along, but he persisted in asking me so I finally decided to give it a try. You see, I'd never actually been on a camping trip as an adult. The only camping excursion I can remember from my childhood was a day trip with the Girl Scouts which ended with me getting sick in the back of a station wagon (pass the Dixie cups as fast as you can, please) and having to cut the trip short. Then again, that's what you get for putting the girl who was prone to car sickness in the very back of a station wagon, facing out the back, with a bunch of other girls.

Nevertheless, the camping trips John and I took managed to leave a few positive impressions: feeding squirrels by hand, listening to Mountain Jays each morning, napping by the lake while the wind blew through the trees, waking up to the smell of campfire coffee, swimming in an icy cold reservoir on a warm summer afternoon, playing gin rummy under the shade of a pine tree, roasting marshmallows and making s'mores, and simply watching the starry sky at night.

After our six-week visit to the hospital in October 2004, John still wanted to go camping. By the time we made our last trip in May 2005, John was a home dialysis patient. That meant we were dialyzing him ourselves with fluid that drained into his abdominal cavity through a port in his stomach and was drained back out a few hours later; we did this four times each day, every day of the week. I found it cumbersome but John was tired of driving to the dialysis clinic three days a week and he wanted the freedom to travel. In other words, he wanted to be able to camp. I was kind of a basket case about dialyzing him at a campsite. The doctors and nurses drill it into you that your environment has to be incredibly sterile. If you've ever been camping then you know that sterile doesn't often describe a campground. But John was adamant, and since we had recently purchased a tent trailer, he figured we'd be clean enough inside of it. Every time we set up the dialysis equipment, I would watch with dread while dust particles floated through the air, absolutely certain that we were going to end up with a contaminated abdominal port and a life-threatening infection.

But it wasn't an infection that ended up threatening his life just a few months later. It would be a phone call on a Sunday afternoon in September 2005 that would take us back to the hospital after a seemingly benign test result.

Chapter 8

THE NOT SO LONG GOODBYE

The last thing we wanted to do was go back to the hospital.

It was a Sunday afternoon when the dialysis center called to tell us that John's latest lab work showed a low platelet count. It was low enough to warrant a call and a recommendation that we go to the hospital and self-admit. Had he not been married, I believe John would have blown off their suggestion and given up the fight. As it was, I still had to give him "the look" and convince him that we should go and see what was happening with his blood work.

John had been a dialysis patient for ten months. During the six-week hospital stay the previous October, John had gained approximately 60 pounds in water weight because his heart wasn't pumping enough blood to his kidneys to allow them to do their job properly. Every time the doctors tried to pull the water weight off through medication, his kidney function would go in the tank. They would then stop the medication and John would regain the weight plus a few additional pounds. It was like yo-yo dieting, but worse. His congestive heart failure had worsened and the medications were no longer keeping up. After almost a month, they finally decided that dialysis was the only effective method for drawing off the fluid. The problem, though, is that once you start dialysis you have to continue; the doctors weren't very clear about that when they started the treatments. They also didn't explain how hard dialysis is on the heart. We didn't know it but we were essentially signing John's death warrant.

As a dialysis patient, John's blood was tested periodically to make sure that the treatments were effective and that nothing else was going on. On this particular occasion, the request to test his blood had come after staff had noticed how tired he was after treatments. I'd gone with John to some of his appointments and stayed with him the whole time. I saw how he and other patients in the center would sleep away their time on the artificial kidney and how weak some of them were when they were done. John, in particular, had grown increasingly tired. In the months leading up to the phone call, John had started using a walker. His legs simply wouldn't support his weight and a cane was no longer sufficient. Dialysis staff had seen his shuffling gait and noticed how weak his speech had become. Sometimes, at the end of his appointments, his voice was barely more than a hoarse whisper. Almost always, after his appointments, he would come home and take a nap in his recliner.

About a week before the call, John and I had celebrated my birthday and it was painfully obvious that he was pushing his limits that day. We had gone to see "Happy Feet" and he had fallen asleep during the movie. Granted, dancing penguins weren't really his thing, but it was more than disinterest that had closed his eyes that afternoon. Later, we met friends at a restaurant for dinner and it was all he could do to stay awake and maintain a conversation. He had shopped for me a few days earlier and I knew that it had taken all of his energy to do it, but that's just who John was: he was a warrior. He had been fighting battles his entire life. There wasn't an enemy he wasn't willing to face and meeting me had just made him all the more valiant. During our numerous hospital stays, he used to tell me that he was fighting hard so that we could have more time together. He would often say that if I hadn't been in his life, he probably would have given up because the pain and discomfort were so severe.

And so it was that the warrior agreed to enter the fray once more after the dialysis center called and told us to go to the hospital that night. Even though I knew we had to go, and even though I had given John "the look," I wasn't any more enthusiastic than he was. If you've ever spent time in a hospital, you know why — nothing happens quickly in a hospital. It's a lot of hurrying up and waiting for everything. You wait to be seen. You wait to be admitted. You wait for your doctor to show up on rounds. You wait for testing. You wait for test results. You wait to be medicated. You wait to be discharged. You have zero control and you are at the mercy of a bunch of people who don't know you from Adam and are being pulled in a hundred different directions by other patients just like you. It can be scary and confusing, and it's the last place you want to be if you're trying to get some rest. On top of all that, it meant that John and I would be separated yet again.

I did what I could to spend as much time with John whenever he was in the hospital but it was never enough. During the week, I would go to work then go straight to the hospital. We would have dinner together and then talk and watch television until about 10:00 p.m. Saying goodnight was always difficult and we drew it out as long as we could. On weekends, I would get to the hospital in the morning and I'd spend all day until the late evening. On Sundays, I would bring the paper and we would read it together, along with all the cooking magazines we subscribed to.

During that lengthy stay in October 2004, I did spend one night with John when he was having an especially bad time. Things had gone from bad to worse with his fluid gain and our requests for a consultation with a nephrologist had been ignored. John was deeply discouraged and I was just getting angry. You see, we weren't your average hospital patients. We were well informed about John's health and I took my responsibility as his partner and caregiver seriously. I had his health and medication history memorized and I could, as one ICU nurse would later tell me, "give report" on John better than some of the other nurses she knew. I also wasn't afraid to fight for him. On one occasion when an emergency room doctor insisted that John had overdosed on his pain medication despite my report that just the opposite had happened, I was on the phone at the nurses' station with John's primary care doctor at 2:00 a.m. demanding that his pain meds be reinstated immediately. So when I saw that John wasn't getting the care he desperately needed in 2004, I spent that night with him and prepared to have him released the next morning. When his doctors showed up with medical students in tow, they found me and John sitting on the edge of his bed, his bag packed, and our eyes red from crying and lack of sleep. Within an hour, doctors had written orders for an ultrasound on John's heart along with a referral for a nephrologist, and he was scheduled for a procedure to have a central line installed which I was invited to observe.

Normally, though, spending the night wasn't necessary. I certainly could have done it any time I wanted and nurses invited me to stay on a number of occasions, but I knew I would be of more help to John if I was well-rested. Even John once told me that one of us had to resume a normal life and it clearly wasn't going to be him during our hospital stays.

On September 18, 2005, we returned to the hospital once more, unaware that it would be our last admit — and the beginning of the last week of John's life.

The two big issues facing John's doctors during that last hospital stay were the low platelet count and his worsening heart failure. To address the low plate-lets, they ordered a bone marrow biopsy; they sus-pected leukemia and wanted to confirm it. For his heart, an MRI was needed. His cardiologist needed a clear idea of why John's heart wasn't pumping to its full capacity. The power behind each pump of his heart was good but the amount of blood being pumped out into his body was low. The MRI would reveal the reason behind the restriction.

There were two theories being discussed: either John's heart was being restricted by scar tissue from his three open heart surgeries or his heart was simply damaged beyond repair from the radiation therapy he had received three decades earlier. If the culprit was scar tissue, doctors could go in and remove it, thereby freeing up his heart to pump more effectively. If his heart was simply bad, the only option was a transplant.

Early in the week, doctors completed the bone marrow biopsy and we prepared for the MRI. Usually, an MRI doesn't require sedation but in John's case, he suffered from extreme claustrophobia. In Vietnam, he had served as a helicopter crew chief and door gunner. He and his crew had been shot down several times but the last time was the worst. Trapped on his back in the wreckage for hours while Vietnamese soldiers came through the area, he laid there as the only survivor among his crew, feigning death so that he wouldn't be taken prisoner. Physically, he would recover, but the emotional wounds never fully healed. For the rest of his life, he would never be comfortable on his back, not even sleeping in bed. His condition would necessitate full anesthesia for the MRI.

A friend of mine was visiting with us when the doctor gave us the test results. They had found no evidence of scar tissue. His heart had simply grown rigid and inflexible over time as a result of the radiation. The doctor left us with a packet of information about heart transplants along with an application for the program. My friend excused herself and left us to discuss our options. Always being ready to fix things, I started looking at the materials and asking John questions. He quickly stopped me, saying he was tired and asking if we could talk about it later. Part of me was panicking because I knew time was of the essence, but I could see he was exhausted. It was also obvious that his body, with its poor circulation, hadn't fully eliminated the anesthesia. John hadn't been fully coherent since the MRI and our discussions about his health had taken place during the tiny windows of opportunity where he was both lucid and energetic.

By the time Thursday rolled around, we had also been given the news that John had, in fact, developed leukemia. *Like he doesn't have enough problems as it is*, I thought. To tell you that we were overwhelmed would be a gross understatement. No wonder John preferred to hide within the stupor of his anesthesia-induced haze. I gladly would have joined him if I could. Instead, I was left to navigate an ocean of fear, confusion, and frustration. Even as I sat next to him in that hospital room, holding his hand, I knew I was losing him. Sometimes, I would try and will him awake so we could talk. I desperately wanted back the man I'd met two years earlier. I simply couldn't reconcile the man I'd known then with the man who was all bundled up in warming blankets in the bed next to me.

As I got ready to leave Thursday night, John's nurse came in and gave him his medication. After she left, we began the long process of saying goodnight. I gathered up my purse and the paperwork that inevitably accumulated each day, and was about to walk out the door when it happened. John called out to me and told me he felt like he was going to be sick. I dropped my things on the chair and got him a pan. As he vomited up his evening medication, he must have aspirated some of it into his lungs because he started to choke and go into respiratory distress. I immediately yelled out into the hallway for help and soon our room was filled with nurses and a respiratory technician. Within minutes, it was barely controlled chaos as they worked to get John's breathing under control. John, I'm certain, was not a happy camper. They had put a breathing mask over his face, something as equally unpleasant as being on his back. He was probably panicking, especially since I couldn't be right next to him to keep him calm. Eventually, I heard one of the nurses tell the others that they were going to have to move him up to the ICU because he needed more care than they could give him on the telemetry ward.

Things didn't get much better once we moved up to the ICU. Once again, we had a large team of staff working on John to improve his breathing. They placed a forced air mask over his nose and mouth to help keep him oxygenated. Through the mask, I could hear John yelling at them to take it off. At that point, I made my way bedside to take his hand and talk him through the process. The doctors were testing blood gases every five minutes, so not only was he trapped under a mask, he was getting pricked and prodded constantly. Eventually, the blood gas tests started coming back normal, the mask was removed, and things started to quiet down in his room. At that point, I decided to spend the night because there was no way I was leaving John in that condition. I settled into the bedside chair, and in between feeding John ice chips throughout the night, we both fell into short periods of napping.

I still remember that Friday morning; it was bright and clear. I woke up, opened the blinds, and went over to sit on the edge of John's bed. I held his hand and we just sat there for a few minutes, neither one of us saying anything. Finally, it was John who broke the silence. "I'm tired, and I just want to go to sleep," he said, and we both knew he wasn't talking about taking a nap. He'd made a decision that morning, and while phrased as a statement, his words actually conveyed a request. John had been fighting so hard and so long and, like any good soldier, he wasn't just giving up; he was requesting permission to be relieved of duty. I know without a doubt that if I'd refused his request and asked him to carry on, he would have complied, but I'd suffered right along with him for 2 ½ years. I had been there through the tests, procedures, and diagnoses. I knew what he had endured, and I knew what faced us if we chose to continue the fight. My sweet man had been a valiant warrior and I loved him too much to put him through any more pain.

"Ok," I whispered, and started to cry.

Chapter 9

A TEMPORARY SOBRIETY

"I'll miss you."

Those were John's next words after I agreed to his request to stop fighting the good fight to stay alive. It was one of the last lucid moments he and I would share.

I think John knew he was dying long before that week. I think he knew it back in February of that year when he surprisingly announced that we could get married in March. He had proposed on March 21st the previous year, on the one-year anniversary of our first date, and suggested we get married in October 2005. He wanted a long engagement, something he'd not had in his prior marriage, but as our anniversary loomed close again he got it in his head that we should get married on that date. A weekend trip to

Reno with our two closest friends sealed the deal as we exchanged wedding vows at the Chapel of the Bells on March 21, 2005.

John claimed it was the ease of remembering just one special anniversary date, but I think there may have been more to it. He was often very protective about what he shared with me. For example, he rarely shared his experiences in Vietnam with me. "You don't need to know those things," he would tell me. Only twice — under the influence of alcohol — did John reveal details from that time in his life, so I have no doubt he believed that details regarding his health, especially any feeling he had that he might have been dying, were best left unspoken.

When the doctor showed up during rounds that Friday morning, we told him we were done. We asked that no further treatments be provided and no more tests be run. He understood our decision and left to inform his staff. I steeled myself for weeks, if not months, of hospice care at our home. I told John I needed to make some phone calls and left for the waiting room. I had barely gotten outside his room when one of the ICU nurses stopped me. She told me the doctor had informed them of John's decision and told them that he would be surprised if John lasted the night. She knew the doctor hadn't said that in front of us and she thought I should know. I remember feeling like time had stopped suddenly. The seconds ticked by in extreme slow motion as I just looked at the nurse and tried to reconcile my assumption that I had weeks to prepare for John's death with the reality that he probably wouldn't survive the next 24 hours. As the two ideas collided in my head, I fell apart. The strength and composure which had served me and John so well for the past 2 ½ years crumbled in that moment. There were no questions to be asked, no demands to be made, and no instructions to be followed — only tears to be cried. Completely undone by that nurse's words, I sagged to the floor.

After a few minutes, the nurse helped me up and I made my way to the waiting room. I still had calls to make but the message was now very different. The first call was the hardest. I dialed the number for one of our closest friends. She was at work, and I hated to bother her there, but I had no choice. I opened my mouth to tell her the news but instead of words, sobs just came pouring out. It took a few minutes to compose myself and tell her what had happened but once I did, she told me not to worry and that she and her husband would be right there. Knowing that help was on the way calmed me down a bit and the rest of the calls were slightly easier. I told friends and family that they needed to get to the hospital that afternoon to say goodbye. Amazingly, everyone I called showed up, even John's cousin from the Bay Area.

The doctor had put in an order for comfort care only, meaning that no life-extending or life-saving measures were to be taken. The only medication that would be administered would be a morphine drip, and I had asked that they hold off on that until everyone had said their goodbyes. Unfortunately, John had been given some other pain medication prior to the order being entered, and he was pretty drowsy by the time friends and family started arriving. As we crowded around his bed, waiting for him to wake up, we began to share our favorite memories of John. We traded stories. We laughed and cried. We hugged and we held hands. Finally, just after his cousin arrived, he opened his eyes. As he took in the sight of his closest friends and family gathered around him, the sweetest look came over his face. It was almost mischievous, as if he was thinking, *You punks! You decided to have a party and didn't even tell me!* I wish I'd had a camera to capture it. Once he was awake, everyone took turns sitting by his side and holding his hand. At one point, I excused myself to use the ladies' room and one of our friends took my place by his side. She took his hand and told John she was taking my place for a few minutes. Through his painkiller haze, he commented, "Oh, no one can ever take her place." Even at the end, he was still my dear, sweet man.

Later that afternoon, John was moved out of the ICU to another floor for the remainder of his comfort care. I spent that night with him and two of my friends stayed, as well. It was then, as we sat together talking in John's room, that I discovered how ill-prepared I was for him to leave me. With all of John's medical issues taking precedence in our life, John and I had never taken the time to update his banking and insurance records after we got married back in March. I wasn't named on his checking account, though he had shared his ATM card and pin number, and I had no clue whether or not he had listed me as the beneficiary on his insurance documents. By this time, John had been on a morphine drip for several hours and it was too late to address the issue. It would prove to be a very costly mistake: John's life insurance payout would end up going to his ex-wife, who was still listed as his beneficiary, and the bank would later force me to return the checking account funds I had withdrawn because I wasn't a signer on that account.

On Saturday, we were visited by a few more friends. One of the nurses who had taken care of us came by to see John, as well. She had heard what happened and wanted to check in. John was always a favorite among the nursing staff. They were never supposed to cherry-pick patients but I think John was usually at the top of their preferred patient list. He was funny and engaging, and always said "please" and "thank you." John loved talking about the shows he watched on the Food Network and he was always quick to share recipes and cooking tips with the nurses. When our small patio garden started bearing fruit, we shared the bounty with the nursing staff—which made us very popular! Because of all the time we had spent in hospitals, we knew how hard the nurses worked and we understood that your assigned nurse could make or break your stay.

As I stood with our former nurse next to John's bed, she told me what to expect as the end drew near. She explained how his body would start to shut down and how his breathing would change. I am forever grateful for the information she shared that day. I had never witnessed death up close and I really didn't know what to expect. Her comments helped me prepare for the end so that I could focus all the more on John and helping him to let go. Before she left, she commented that I wasn't having John turned in his bed. I told her I didn't want him disturbed any more than was necessary. She understood my reasoning, but then explained that the turning process actually helps hasten the end of life and is an act of mercy once a patient is so close to death. Eventually, I decided to allow staff to turn him every few hours but whenever they came in, I had to leave the room; not because they asked me, but because it was too painful to watch. It's hard to describe because it doesn't sound like much is happening and there doesn't seem to be much that's hard to watch: staff come in, they move the support pillows under the patient from one side to the other, rearrange the pillow under the patient's head so that they are facing the opposite direction, and that's it. However, that little bit of disturbance is enough to elicit a response of sorts from the patient. I could see it in John's face and hear it in his breathing that it was disruptive. I knew it was supposed to be, and that there was a good reason for it, but I couldn't just stand there and watch them hurry the dying process along.

Whenever we had visitors, we always made sure to include John in our conversations. Nurses had told us that the sense of hearing remains intact until death, so we used that to our advantage. We encouraged and comforted John with our words. We told jokes and relived memories with him. Sometimes, his breathing would change and he would make sounds, almost like groans, in response to something we said, as if he were trying to join the conversation. His facial expressions went through numerous changes once he was on the morphine drip, and it looked like he was working through a lifetime of experiences and memories. For a while, he looked frustrated and anxious, almost like he was angry. At one point, his face took on a sad expression and it seemed to me that he was thinking about everything and everyone he would miss here in the world. Eventually, it appeared he was done and his face took on a quiet and peaceful look. The internal struggle had ended, allowing him to rest and wait for the end to come.

Around 1:00 a.m. on Sunday, I noticed that John's breathing had slowed significantly and the end appeared to be approaching. We still had a couple of friends visiting with us, and they were debating whether they should stay or go home and return in the morning. No sooner had we talked about it than we noticed the change in his breathing. The three of us stood around John's bed, holding his hands, stroking his hair and face — doing whatever we could to let him know he was loved and that he wasn't going to die alone. We told him it was ok to let go and to finally get some rest. He had fought a long, hard fight and it was ok to stop struggling. He began the death gasps just then, signaling the final stage. It looks just like it sounds. John's mouth opened and closed, silently trying to take in air, much like a goldfish when it lands outside its watery home. Even though I was expecting it, it was horrific to watch. It looked like he was suffocating. I remember I prayed then. I don't know that I've ever prayed so hard for anyone. It felt like the veins in my forehead would explode. I begged God to take John quickly so that he wouldn't have to suffer any longer. One of our friends had just commented on what a fighter John was, and that he might hang on for a while longer. I couldn't stand to see John like this, and even though I wasn't a Christ-follower at that time, I know God heard my prayer and answered it.

Less than 10 minutes later, John breathed his last. It came suddenly and quietly. One moment he was gasping, and in the next he was still, his eyes having come slightly open. Death, even under the cover of a morphine drip, is dramatic and noticeable. You don't need to hear someone breathe their last in order to know that life has left the body. The stillness and lack of life are unmistakable. As soon as the heart stops beating and blood stops circulating, a gray, ashy pallor takes over the face. It's odd what we tend to think about when we witness death. I clearly remember thinking, *It's not like you see on television.* What a random thing. Of course it wouldn't be like television, but that was the only place where I'd seen death. It was my only frame of reference. It was logical yet totally ridiculous all at the same time.

We called the nurse, who came in and checked for any signs of life; she, in turn, called the doctor. When he arrived, he confirmed what we knew and announced the time of death. After so much struggling to keep John alive, I felt utterly lost as we packed up our things to leave the hospital one last time. *It couldn't be over just like that*, I thought. *There must be something I can do for him.* Leaving him and walking out of that room felt so final; I couldn't comprehend it. If my friends hadn't been there to help shepherd me out of John's room, I'm not sure I would have left. That was the shock setting in, I'd later realize, a stupor that would last through the memorial service a week later.

Death is a sobering experience. A couple of weeks after John's death, I was putting on make-up and suddenly noticed how much older I looked. It wasn't a wrinkle thing; it was a soul thing. My eyes looked ancient in that moment. I couldn't erase what I'd seen and I couldn't forget what I'd been through. It was all there, indelibly burned into my memory banks. For the first few weeks, I had lots of people to share those memories with, but pretty soon life returned to its normal rhythms and I was left alone to process through my grief.

I'd always thought of myself as being pretty resilient. Nothing much ever got me down and I always managed to rebound quickly. When John died, I immediately started taking care of all the business that needs attention in the wake of someone's passing. There were creditors to notify, bank accounts to close, and insurance claims to file. I cleaned out his closet and donated shoes and clothing. I collected all of his old jewelry, including our wedding rings, and took it to a local pawn shop to help pay for some immediate expenses I had looming over my head. Wondering if a grief support group might be helpful, I attended a session at a local hospital one night. I was taken aback at how fresh some of the women's grief was, even after many months and, in some cases, years. Sensing I had moved beyond a need for the group, I left and never returned.

Looking back, I wasn't processing through my grief at all. I was simply sweeping it under a rug. I certainly wasn't going through it, looking at it, and dealing with it. Counseling would have been in order at that time, but just like with my first marriage, it simply didn't occur to me. I missed John terribly but I can remember only one moment of really letting those emotions come to the surface. I was lying on our bed and I just kept crying out, "Damn you for leaving me!" as I pounded the mattress with my fist over and over again. The hours right after getting home from work were the worst. That's when John and I used to sit together and debrief our days over drinks and snacks before dinner. After he died, I'd walk in the house and it would be so quiet. I'd just pace around the house not knowing what to do with myself. Sometimes, I'd start talking out loud as if to share with him. It seemed to help a bit but never enough. Eventually, I stopped doing it.

Because I was ignoring my grief instead of engaging with it, it was easy to mistakenly believe that I was emotionally healthy and ready to move on. When you refuse to address the root causes of your addiction, sobriety will only be a temporary condition. I hadn't dealt with any of my baggage; consequently, it was dealing with me. I was incredibly lonely, so it was easy for the enemy to lure me back into addiction—just four months after John died, I was back online looking for companionship. It only took a couple of months for me to meet someone new.

His name was "Jeff" and he lived in a small tourist community nestled in the Angeles National Forest in Southern California. He drove up one weekend to visit me and we quickly ended up in bed together. One of God's purposes in giving us the gift of sexual intimacy is, in fact, comfort, but He always intended it to be used that way in the context of marriage. When King David and Bathsheba's son died, David went in to her, as his wife, and they found comfort in each other's arms.[9] I was seeking comfort, as well, but I was looking for it in the arms of a near stranger.

Over the next 18 months, I would settle back into old habits and patterns of behavior. There would be several men, some married and some single, who would pass through my arms. One was significantly younger and called himself "Gabriel" because he told me he always entered someone's life just when they needed an angel. He was probably the most blatant representative of the enemy and the counterfeit pleasures he offers that I encountered during that time. I threw caution to the wind with another partner and engaged in unprotected sex, resulting in a potential exposure to herpes. With yet another, I explored the world of male chastity, a behavior similar to dominant/submissive lifestyles.

"Richard" was the most normal date I had during that time. He was very much my physical type: tall and barrel-chested with a goatee and a nice smile. Both of us had been widowed and, incredibly, our spouses had passed away within a week of each other. We saw each other every night for almost a week and he was in as much of a rush as me to get into a new relationship. By our 6th or 7th date, he was asking me about my ring size. Just a week later, though, my interest in Richard cooled substantially. He was a nice man, polite and gentlemanly, and I think that was my problem—he was too nice. The men I'd been spending time with hadn't treated me well at all but Richard treated me like gold. I'd had to work to get others to pay attention to me; consequently, Richard's affections felt almost like smothering. That following weekend, I told Richard I needed my space and called things off. There was no hiding his surprise and disappointment. Unfortunately, he was simply one of several nice and decent men that I would hurt because of my brokenness.

Chapter 10

"WE'VE BEEN HERE ALL ALONG"

Even though you planned evil against me, God planned good to come out of it. – **Genesis 50:20**

B y the time August 2007 rolled around, I'd spent almost seven years engaged in sexual sin and online dating addiction. My brief and sobering marriage to John wasn't enough to heal my past and break my addiction. It had been merely a temporary fix, and as soon as it was gone I went right back to my old ways.

That's how addiction works. We discover something that makes us feel good, or gives us a high, and as we repeat that experience, we create neural pathways in our brain. We literally rewire our brain as we seek out those pleasurable experiences over and over again. No matter how many times we may want to stop, we are unable to do so. No matter how sincere we are when we promise to never do something again, we are unable to keep that promise. Just talk to anyone who's ever been addicted to anything—drugs, alcohol, food, gambling, sex, or something else—and they'll tell you how impossible it was to stop. In my particular case, it was only by the grace of God that I was delivered from addiction. Sadly, though, my initial deliverance was only superficial and temporary because I didn't see my addiction for what it was. Ironically, I simply substituted God as the new object of my addictive attention. I threw myself headlong into relationship with Him and never dealt with the underlying issues that had led to my addiction in the first place.

As only God can do, He used the very thing which had held me captive for so long to set me free; He revealed Himself to me through a dating relationship. "Alex" was managing a small casual dining restaurant at the time and had served in the Marines as a young man. One of his sons was also serving as a Marine, and shortly after we met in person Alex and his family got word that his son had been critically injured by an IED. That tragic event would open the door for God to get close to me.

Alex and I hadn't yet been on a real date. We had only met a few times at his restaurant to chat. Our first date was postponed even further when he flew back east to Bethesda to be with his son who had been flown there for treatment. The prognosis was bleak and doctors were encouraging the family to say their goodbyes due to the traumatic brain injury inflicted by the bomb blast. But Alex and his family were Christians and they were adamant that God could, and would, heal his son. They began praying over his son and within the week that he spent there, God began to work a miracle. The changes were small but significant, and every bit of improvement was credited to God's grace and mercy.

Alex and I were in constant contact while he was away. He updated me on his son's condition and the improvements he was making. I was as supportive as I could be long-distance and prayed as best I knew how at that time. We made plans to meet at his home when he returned from Bethesda, plans that included me spending the night. It was late when he returned, and not surprisingly, we wasted little time getting into bed. Once again, comfort was the underlying motivation; Alex needed it and I wanted to provide it. Sex was simply the wrong method since we weren't married. At that time in my life, sex was the only way I knew how to relate to men. I wasn't especially attracted to Alex but I was attracted to what he represented: attention, affection, meaning and purpose for my life, and the chance for me to feel powerful and in control of something for a while. It was always about the chase and the conquest. Getting a man into bed, and then satisfying him, was the high. I was always willing to deny my own preferences and desires in order to get my fix. I was blinded to how poorly I was being treated. I tolerated — even welcomed — shabby treatment as long as I got what I wanted in the dating relationship.

As our dating continued, I was introduced to other family members. I met another of Alex's sons along with Alex's two brothers and sister. One of his brothers was a pastor and he and his wife ran a home-based church on the weekend for friends and family. I was invited to attend several of those services, along with a few prayer meetings where friends and family gathered to pray for Alex's son. I always went, not because I was especially interested in God, but simply to support Alex and spend time with him. In my addiction, I only really cared about meeting my own needs and if being supportive for Alex was the means to that satisfaction, then so be it.

I had no idea God was about to turn my addiction on its head and use it for His glory.

Alex and I had been dating for about a month and a half when he decided it was time to have a talk. He wanted to discuss our future and told me that he wasn't sure our relationship was going to go any further. Alex wanted a spouse who would share his faith and be willing to serve in ministry alongside him. He knew I wasn't a believer, and he knew what the Bible said about light having nothing to do with darkness and a believer having nothing to do with an unbeliever, in terms of a marriage relationship. He'd been thinking about this for a while and had even broached the topic to his pastor brother. He told Alex, "She may not be a believer, but she continues to show up." He understood that simply showing up in the presence of God was half the battle and I believe that his brother's encouragement was the primary reason Alex continued to see me for as long as he did.

As I sat there listening to Alex, all I could think was, *I'm losing him.* I didn't give a rip about attending church with him, or serving with him, or having a personal relationship with Christ. I just wanted to continue seeing Alex. That was my motivation as I launched into a marathon prayer session later that night. I had dinner plans with friends and the drive to their house took almost an hour. I spent the entire drive asking God for one thing: to make me into the kind of woman Alex wanted to be with. I am absolutely certain that as soon as God heard me utter those words, He smiled and said, "Oh beloved, I am SO going to answer that prayer!"

The next day was Sunday, and Alex and I attended church at his brother's home. It wasn't the first time I'd been to services with them but it *was* the first time it really made an impression. I sat there watching Alex's brother and sister-in-law teach that morning and noticed something unusual. They were sitting in two separate chairs right next to each other, almost touching shoulders. That, in itself, wasn't unusual but the bright light that seemed to be shining between them — that was very unusual. I remember listening to them but not really hearing them; I was fascinated with that light. I kept staring at that small space between them, trying to figure out the source of the light. And while I can't recall the topic of their message that Sunday, I remember that I felt like information was being downloaded into my brain. Insight after insight filled my head that morning and I felt energized in a way that I never had before. After their service, I couldn't wait to get home; there was an urgency to write down everything that had been dumped into my head. I sat down at my dining room table and began to write. Page after page, the thoughts tumbled out, almost faster than I could write. I turned another page and wrote, "Being Saved." And that's when I hit the brakes.

I sat there, puzzled, as I wondered why that was such a sticking point for me. There had been a few occasions during the church services and prayer meetings when his friends and family had asked me if I was a Christian. I knew what they meant and my stock answer was always, "Well, I was raised Catholic." I knew that wasn't the same thing as being born again or being saved, but I was hesitant to really talk to them about it because they were into things like praying in tongues and that just seemed weird to me at the time; I also felt intimidated by it. At one meeting, Alex's brother shared how Alex's daughter-in-law, while in Bethesda with her injured husband, received Christ and immediately started praying in tongues. They all praised God, and her, and you could tell they were all so proud of her. I heard that story and was afraid that if I didn't pray in tongues when I was saved, that I wouldn't really be saved and I would be seen as not having done it right. I already felt a bit like an outcast in their presence because Alex had told me early on to not let his family know we were sleeping together. We were keeping this dirty little secret and hearing about his amazing daughter-in-law just made things worse. There was no way I was willing to be vulnerable in their presence.

But as I sat there in my dining room, pen poised above the page in my journal, God reminded me of something. In my junior year of high school, I had attended a Warehouse Ministries event with some friends. When the pastor gave the altar call, I raised my hand and invited Jesus into my heart. Twenty-seven years had gone by, and that memory had been long buried under a mountain of sin until God decided to resurrect it for me in that moment. Immediately, I felt something give way inside me and it was like a fog suddenly lifted. I saw in my mind a picture of the Godhead surrounding me, the faces of God the Father, Jesus the Son, and the Holy Spirit positioned around me about an arm's length away. In my heart, I heard them whisper, "We've been here all along, this close. You just couldn't see us."

I've done it before, I thought, *and I can do it again.* At the age of 16, when I invited Jesus into my life, I didn't understand what I had done. Technically, I'd

been saved then but now I wanted to make that decision with purpose and intention. I wanted to know
exactly what it meant to be born again and I wanted
to understand the Gospel message. I knew I needed to
talk to someone about it, and I knew just who to ask.

My coworker was attending a church called New
Song and I figured if anyone could hook me up with
a pastor, it was her. I approached her one day and
asked if there was someone at her church I could talk
to about what it meant to be saved. She made a phone
call for me and found out that the senior pastor was
away on a retreat but the family and children's pastor
was available. Steve was very down to earth and easy
to talk with. I told him about my high school experience and how I now wanted to give my life to God
with a full understanding of what I was doing and
why. He explained the Gospel message to me and
gave me a few Bible verses to read through. While I
was eager to take this next step, I knew I wanted to do
it in the privacy of my home. My confession of faith
was going to be messy and I really didn't want to do
that in front of someone I'd only met a few minutes
earlier.

Steve asked me to send him an email letting him know how it went and I promised I would. I drove home as quickly as I could safely manage and then beelined it for my bedroom. I sat down on the floor next to my bed and began reading through the verses Steve had given me. *We have all fallen short of the glory of God,* one read. *The wages of sin is death,* declared another. I read through all of them once, then twice. After reading through them a third time, I got on my knees, leaned on my bed and began to confess a lifetime of poor choices, foolish decisions, and selfish behavior. All the years of sexual sin came pouring out — proud moments, angry moments, and just plain dumb moments. It all rushed out amid sobs and apologies to God. No longer did I want to do life my way. It all seemed so wrong in that moment and I wanted something better: I wanted to surrender to God and do life on His terms.

After a while, my tears subsided and my breathing returned to normal. Kneeling there by my bed, I realized quite suddenly that I felt happy. Not just kinda happy or superficially happy. I'm talking about deep-down, ecstatic, feeling like I could fly, happy. I looked at the alarm clock on my nightstand. October 16, 2007, 6:20 PM — the date and time stamp of my spiritual rebirth.

The next day at work, I approached another coworker who I knew was part of a prayer group that met each week at the office. I asked her if the group was still meeting. She gave me kind of a funny look, as if trying to figure out my intentions. Cautiously, she replied that yes, they still met. Then it was my turn to be cautious, wondering how she would respond to my next question. I asked if I could join them the next time they met. It was the last question she expected and I was probably the last person she expected to ask it, but join them I did, and I told them about my decision. In Luke 15:7, God tells us that there is more rejoicing in heaven over the one sinner who repents than over the remainder who need no repentance. The ladies in that prayer group rejoiced over me that day, celebrating with all of heaven. As we closed in prayer, I did something I'd never done before—I prayed out loud in a group setting. In all the prayer meetings I'd attended with Alex, I had never dared open my mouth. But that day, with those ladies, God filled me with courage and loosened my tongue.

That same week, Alex and I made plans to get together. I showed up at his house, excited to share my news. I expected an enthusiastic response in light of the conversation we'd had a week earlier, but when I told him I'd given my life to God, I barely got a lukewarm reply. I was a little confused and said so. He told me he was happy for me, but you never would have known it by his body language and facial expression. Disappointed, I left early and began to wonder if Alex and I had a future together.

Over the next week, I noticed that my feelings for Alex began to change. For starters, I no longer felt ok about sleeping with him. What's interesting about that change of heart is how I came to the realization—I hadn't read it in the Bible yet and I hadn't heard about it in a sermon, but what I did have was a piece of God in my heart. When I invited Jesus into my life, He put His very own Spirit inside me to direct me, and part of that direction included a conviction of sin—a revelation of things I needed to stop doing.

I also began noticing how poorly Alex was treating me. When I would go over to his house to visit, and his son answered the door, Alex never got up out of his chair to greet me. He always expected me to go over to him. Additionally, I could no longer reconcile Alex keeping our physical relationship a secret with his profession of faith as a Christian. Despite all that, I was praying that God would improve things between us. The more I prayed, though, the worse things got and the more I noticed how much I no longer enjoyed being with Alex. After two weeks of prayer, I finally realized that God wasn't going to fix our relationship. It was then my turn to have a talk with Alex. We met for lunch one day and I told him that I felt like God was moving us in two different directions. He seemed a little surprised by my news and expressed a desire to continue dating, but by that time I was ready to move on and start my new life with God.

Chapter 11

FROM HEATHEN TO CHRISTIAN—SORT OF

Approximately one month after giving my life to God, I was baptized at New Song Church in front of my friends, both old and new.

There are a lot of misconceptions about baptism. Some people think it's optional in the Christian life. Others think it's through baptism that we are saved and reborn. Yet others feel it's enough to have been baptized as a baby. There's a lot of teaching about baptism and I'm not going to try and review it all for you here. What I will tell you, though, is how I processed my own baptism. I initially did it because the pastors at New Song encouraged me to do so as the next step in my walk with God. They explained it was something a Christ-follower did to publicly associate themselves with Jesus; it was an external demonstration of an internal decision. In full immersion water baptism, my old life would be buried with Christ and I would be raised a new creation through His own resurrection from death. My old life had been such a train wreck. I was looking forward to burying it and living out my new life.

While the actual day of my baptism was certainly special and memorable, it was in the months following that event when I really began to understand the impact. After having spent so many years in sexual sin, baptism represented more than just an affiliation with Jesus. For me, I felt *literally* washed clean from all of that sin. In the months after my baptism, God really began to speak to me about what a treasure I was in His sight. A commitment to remain pure and not return to my old life grew strong in my heart as God told me over and over that I was a new creation. The desire to spend time online had disappeared the night I gave my life to God and all I wanted to do was spend time with Him.

I went a little crazy at first, building my collection of Bibles. One of my friends from the workplace prayer group gave me my first Bible, then that same group gave me a study Bible the day of my baptism. After that, I bought several more on my own. I loved spending time in the Christian bookstore; I was like a kid in a candy shop. I literally wanted one of everything. The energy I had poured into my former life was redirected into my relationship with God. I read His Word, I journaled, and I did word studies. My dining room table was rarely used for dining. It was usually covered in Bibles, reference materials, and notebooks.

At New Song, I joined a women's Bible study group. I took every discipleship class they offered. When one of the pastors approached me about serving in the hospitality ministry, I agreed. My responsibilities included the coordination of volunteers for ushering, communion, greeting, and the coffee cart. Pretty soon, I was there every Sunday, helping with setup tasks as well as tear down. Several months in, however, I began to burn out. Unfamiliar with the concept of healthy boundaries, I had said "yes" to everything that was offered because I thought that's what a good Christian did. Not only was I burning out, I was getting frustrated and angry. I hadn't been walking with God for very long, but I knew enough to know that serving out of obligation, with a resentful heart, wasn't honoring to Him.

I eventually mentioned it in my women's group and told them I wanted to step down. I felt guilty about it, like I was letting down the church and the pastors, and even God. Instead of judging or condemning me, wiser women than me told me the healthiest and most courageous thing I could do was step down. They encouraged me to speak with the senior pastor and resign my volunteer position. The following week, I did just that. Even though I was worried about his response, I knew it was the right thing to do. Our pastor couldn't have been more understanding. He knew it was the wisest course of action, as well, and he trusted that God would fill the vacancy with someone who really wanted to serve in that way — and He did. The woman who filled in for me was super gifted when it came to hospitality. Under her guidance, the hospitality ministry really looked and felt hospitable, but she never would have been able to exercise her gifting had I not stepped aside and left a vacancy.

As my first two years of Christianity progressed, I pursued God the way I had pursued men earlier in my life. I chased hard and rejoiced whenever I understood a piece of Scripture or received an insight because it felt like I was somehow "conquering" God.

147

I wouldn't have described it that way at the time, but looking back I can see that's what I was doing. In a very real sense, I was still seeking the high I used to get from dating; because of that, my faith was a shallow one and I was content to simply pursue head knowledge. I had a consumer mentality and just wanted to be fed. In fact, at one point during those first couple of years, I started visiting another church on Saturdays and came close to leaving New Song. Everything about that other church was so different from New Song, including their size, their teaching and preaching style, and their praise and worship. There was an immediate emotional response in my heart and I quickly decided that it was in my best interest to join that church. Fortunately, God put a very wise woman in my path who asked some tough questions and got me to think through my decision with wisdom and discernment.

Not only was I relating to God in my old mentality, I was operating under a couple of misconceptions about what it meant to be a Christian. I mistakenly thought that since I had laid my old life to rest, everything about me was instantly new and different and I was ready to rock 'n roll in my life with God. In my naiveté, I believed that all of my old hurts, habits, and hang-ups were gone and that I was now equipped to deal with life in an entirely new way. That particular misconception would eventually lead me to believe that I could once again delve into the realm of online dating and do so responsibly and wisely. After all, I reasoned, I would be looking for a Christian man — but not all Christians are created equal, and that would prove to be my undoing.

I also didn't realize that life with God was going to be a process. I honestly believed that some kind of internal switch had been flipped and things would be smooth sailing from that point forward; consequently, I didn't think I had to put much effort into my new life. When things didn't go well or when I didn't respond as I thought I should, I was sorely disappointed in myself. Believing that God was upset and disappointed with me, I was often riddled with guilt. I wanted to get things right, right out of the gate, and I would beat myself up when I didn't.

One night, after an especially challenging day at work, I came home and slumped down next to an oversized chair in my living room. As I sat on the floor staring at a decorative cross on the wall, I broke down crying, thinking about all the ways I was falling short of what I thought God expected of me. I was constantly criticizing myself, picking apart my behavior, and sliding into self-condemnation. It was an exhausting way to live, and on the floor that night, I wondered why I had so much grace for everyone else and so little for myself. *Why*, I thought, *do I have such a hard time receiving God's love?*

In response to my question, God asked one of His own, "How can you receive love from Someone you're so afraid of?" *Excellent question*, I thought. He was right, after all; I was terrified of Him. I was afraid that He was watching me, shaking His head and wondering when I was going to get my act together. I believed He was just waiting to strike me down at any moment and that's why I was always so quick to beat myself up. I figured if God saw that I was doing a good job of chastising myself, He would go easier on me. In my 45 years on this earth, I hadn't received a whole lot of truly unconditional love. In my mind, I believed God loved me but my heart wasn't buying it. My defenses were up, ready to protect myself if and when God decided to unleash His wrath and punishment.

I couldn't relax in my relationship with God, just like I hadn't been able to really rest in my first marriage. I had to be on guard for when my husband would nitpick the decisions I made and I thought God was standing by, ready to do the same thing. I wasn't comfortable being vulnerable with God, either. What if He failed me or left me? After all, that's what had happened with John. In fact, by this time in my life the three people who had meant the most to me – and had offered me the most unconditional love – had all been taken away. My grandma, my dad, and John had all died and there was no way I was going to risk loving and getting hurt like that ever again.

Instead of investing my heart in a personal relationship with Jesus, I invested my energy in being good for Him. I was busy as a Christian. I spent my time serving, studying, reading, memorizing, and journaling. None of those things in and of themselves are bad. They are all disciplines which are encouraged as part of our growth in the Christian faith. But when that's all you're doing, you're missing the mark by a long shot, especially if you're doing it to be good for God like I was.

God's grace was still a foreign concept to me, as was His unconditional love; that's what happens when you relate to Jesus from your head and not your heart. You can go years in that condition and you can fool a lot of people like that. I looked pretty healthy, emotionally and spiritually. Things were clicking along in my faith walk and I hadn't yet been tested with any challenges or trials. People often commented on what a dramatic change I had undergone, but little did they know that the change was merely a superficial one. Anyone can look good for a while, under relatively easy circumstances, but eventually the façade is challenged and when it is, it invariably crumbles.

Externally, I looked like a good Christian, but inside I was a train wreck because I still hadn't dealt with my past. That, coupled with my misconceptions about following Jesus, would have devastating consequences.

About 18 months into my Christian walk, I began playing with fire. It would just be a matter of time before I got burned.

I was living under the impression that because I hadn't felt a desire to look at an online dating website in a year and a half, I had been supernaturally healed of that desire. That's what I called it—a desire, not an addiction. Sometimes, I went so far as to call it an obsession, but the word addiction didn't really enter my mind. Desire was such a benign word. It gave the impression that I could stop it or control it at any time, and that's how the enemy got me.

When I signed up for eHarmony the first time, I made sure my profile highlighted my faith and I set my match parameters to look for men who shared that faith. I figured I couldn't go wrong if I wrapped the entire experience in a spiritual blanket. There was some of the old excitement, but there was also a measure of caution and uncertainty about what I was doing. Deep down, I knew I was courting trouble but I plowed ahead anyway. I was on the site for about a week and then got a major case of cold feet and cancelled my membership. A few months later, I decided to give it another try. I reinstated my profile and started looking through the matches eHarmony sent.

After a couple of unsuccessful dates, I was frustrated enough to stay off of eHarmony for almost a year. During that time, I briefly dated a gentleman I'll call "Robert". We had gotten to know one another as part of a group of single friends who met regularly for dinner. Robert was a really decent guy; he was just really shy with women. Because I had next to no experience with meeting men outside of a dating website, I was a really poor judge of whether or not someone was interested in me, but it certainly seemed as though Robert liked me. On one occasion, a group of us had gotten together and I had asked if there was any dip to go with the chips the guys had just set out. Robert said, "Uh, just a sec," and then disappeared into the garage. Figuring he had gone to get a jar from their garage pantry, the rest of us resumed our conversation. Sometime later, Robert reappeared with a shopping bag. I looked at him and said, "Did you just go to the grocery store for that dip?" Sheepishly, he nodded his head. I couldn't believe it. He had driven to the store to get dip just because I had casually asked about it.

Over time, we started talking more and eventually made plans to spend a day together in San Francisco. That day in the Bay Area was the beginning of our dating life together. It was both weird and refreshing. I was in unfamiliar territory because I hadn't met him online and was unsure how to behave with him, but taking the online piece out of the equation also gave our dating a fresh and normal feel for me. Perhaps if I'd been more of a Christ-follower in my heart instead of such a Christian in name only, things might have turned out differently for us. Instead, my past and all its junk reared its ugly head. I wanted more of a commitment from Robert and started to put pressure on the relationship. I began to resent him for what I saw as a lack of leadership on his part. Pride and self-righteousness rose to the surface; fear joined the party, as well. *What would people think of us as a couple?* I wanted to be with someone who was biblically knowledgeable and could speak about it with authority and confidence. I couldn't see myself dating someone I perceived as inferior to me.

It's ugly and embarrassing to see those thoughts in black and white now. At the time, though, I couldn't see or appreciate the gift God had given me in Robert. A couple of months later, I pulled a 180 and suddenly ended the dating relationship. It was me and Richard all over again. It was me calling the shots, trying to control the situation and mucking up someone else's life. It was awful, and in my wake Robert was left to pick up the pieces and try to make sense of it all.

Dating Robert had been a very Forrest Gump and Jenny kind of experience for me. I could easily have pictured Robert telling me, as Forrest told Jenny, "I may not be a smart man, Jenny, but I know what love is."[10] And just like Jenny, in the presence of genuine, unconditional love, I got scared and ran away. I couldn't let anyone love me because I hadn't yet learned to love myself. I still believed I was a "less than" person; I wanted someone I perceived as "more than" to make me complete. Anything else would feel like settling, and I'd done enough of that in my lifetime.

That's why my next husband, Paul, would be so attractive. He would look like a savior — the answer to all my prayers — because I hadn't yet come to grips with all of my brokenness and my desperate need for Jesus. But all of that was about to change.

Chapter 12

UNTIL DEATH DO US PART, TAKE 3

I met my third husband in 2010 during my third membership with eHarmony. At the time, I had a great little life in Folsom. I lived in a comfortable, one-bedroom apartment that was nicely appointed with features like crown moulding, a fireplace, and a large kitchen. Getting that apartment had been a total God-thing. I had been looking for a one-bedroom place and after visiting this particular complex because it was located right across the street from my office, I was told that one-bedroom units were extremely hard to come by; as soon as they came open, they were snatched up. I left my name and number that Tuesday and continued my search. The following Saturday, I went out to run a few errands and felt like I should stop back by the complex and see if anything had come open. I got there about an hour after they had opened and asked if any units had become available. As it turned out, a one-bedroom unit had just been surrendered an hour before I got there. They walked me over and showed me the location. It was an upstairs unit, which I wanted, and it overlooked a small greenbelt near the front of the complex. *Perfect*, I thought. I took the apartment and a little less than a month later, I moved in.

Not only did I have a great place to live, I had a great place to work. I was employed as an operations director and had about seven years invested with the company. I supervised a staff of 12 and coordinated special projects for our division. I had a private office facing the walking path and nature area behind our building, affording me a terrific view. I loved the people I worked with and the job was interesting and challenging. That job had been a blessing from God, as well. After working with the company for only a year, the owners created a mid-level management position for me, the first in their organization.

My church life was equally blessed. That year, I had the privilege of leading a couple of Bible studies for a small group of single women. Neither study topic had a prepared lesson plan available for it, but with God's leading I created the curriculum from scratch for both studies using existing reading material. It was an amazing experience to go through the creative process with God and I loved every minute of it. In between the two studies, God prompted me to suggest a series of summer activities to put legs to our faith and action to what we had studied. We called it the Summer of Service, and it included several opportunities for folks to serve the community. Groups of us put together brown bag lunches and walked different areas of the city looking for homeless men and women to feed and serve. We collected pantry items for a local food bank. And, we served a local women's shelter/rehabilitation center by taking the residents and their children out on a couple of excursions. All of that opened the door to a community outreach ministry which was poised to take off that year. I was making connections in the community with other service organizations, and had just recently spoken with the manager of an abortion alternatives center about how our church could partner with their facility.

By the time I met Paul, I was enjoying a bounty of God's blessings. I was rich in ways I'd never imagined. Having always considered myself a solitary person, I was surprised by how much I enjoyed the relationships God brought my way. As I filled my life with the things of Him, He filled my social calendar. Every week, it seemed, I had at least a couple of meetings with women from New Song and I enjoyed countless opportunities to pray with and for them. During the 2 ½ years in my apartment, I hosted numerous dinner parties ranging in size from 2 to 12, with guests that included the closest of friends and total strangers. God blessed me and made me a blessing to others. He was helping me to live out a directive I'd often heard Him whisper to me during my morning walks to "feed people, spiritually and materially." I was dead center in the middle of God's will for my life and I was about to toss it all aside — home, career and ministry — for yet another dating relationship.

Proverbs 3:5 says that we are not to lean on our own understanding, and Proverbs 20:25 reads, "It is a trap for a man to say rashly, 'It is holy!' and after the vows to make inquiry." Those verses would have saved me a lot of heartache and trouble back in 2010 as I got involved with Paul. Though, truth be told, I probably would have ignored them just like I ignored every other red flag that came up in our dating. I was absolutely bent on being with him and I was

convinced that God was leading me into it. I doubt anything or anyone would have been able to change my mind at that time.

Paul looked really good on paper. He had a good job as an operations manager with Boeing. He was renting a two-story home. He had not one, but three, vehicles. He professed a solid faith in Christ and told me he was looking for a godly woman. I took him at his word, which is all you can really do online, but then I continued to take him at his word even after we met and started spending time together. In 1 John 4:1, we read that we are to "test all things" and not just assume that because someone says they are godly that they really are.

You can't really get to know someone through weekend visits. You need to spend time with them. You need to see them at their worst, not just their best. You need to meet their friends and family. You need to see how they steward all that God has given them: their health, finances, home, vehicles, money, time, relationships, and their job. I didn't visit Paul's job site until after I had married him and moved to Washington. I didn't meet his daughter until after we married. I didn't learn the truth about his past until we were married. I didn't discover the truth about his health until after we were *separated*. Trust me when I tell you this is not the way you want to do marriage.

I saw the way he managed his home before I married him but I didn't see it as a red flag. Instead, I saw it as a reason to be with him. He needed me, I reasoned. The stresses and messes in his life didn't appear as warning signs for me. I saw them as doors of opportunity where I could improve his life and take care of him. I met a handful of his friends during one visit when we all attended church together — one time. That wasn't nearly enough to really get to know them and evaluate the health of their friendship.

When Paul flew down to visit me, he always paid for everything. He treated me well and I loved being spoiled. I would later discover that buying me things and taking me places were the *only* ways Paul knew how to invest in another person. He never learned how to engage in a relationship emotionally and spiritually, so he tried to make up for it in material ways. Paul was a master at buying love. He paid for my new cell phone while we were dating and bought me a Jacques Lemans watch for my birthday. My flights to Washington were on his dime. There were no monetary restrictions when we went shopping for engagement and wedding rings. He even made it clear after we got engaged that he didn't want me to work once we were married. He would pay for everything, including my bills.

I saw Paul as my answer to everything. I thought God was giving me every desire of my heart all rolled into one man. Paul was 14 years older than me, well within the age range I had always sought. He was making good money. He took me places and bought me things. He promised to take care of me. I couldn't have articulated it at the time, but in Paul I had found the very dynamic I thought would satisfy me in setting myself up to only date married men years before. With Paul, though, I wouldn't be the other woman; I would be the wife. Totally convinced that this was the right thing for me, I refused to see his bad behavior for what it was.

When Paul told me that he didn't want to schedule time with my friends during our weekend visits, I agreed. It didn't sit well with me but I didn't put up much of a fight. I justified it in my mind and went along with his request. His resistance to my request that we not spend the night under the same roof, even in separate rooms, was a little concerning but I didn't see it as a major problem. Missing a couple of pre-marriage counseling classes and rushing through his homework were excused as minor infractions in my mind. I was disappointed when Paul wasn't able to finish paying for my engagement ring in the time-frame promised, but I didn't make a fuss about it. When my friends asked me about the lack of a ring, I made an excuse and covered for Paul, saying we had agreed to put money towards other wedding expenses first. Only one friend spoke up and said something about Paul's behavior. Again, I made an excuse for Paul and told her that he wasn't like that the rest of the time.

We were married on November 6, 2010. The neediness that I thought would diminish once the wedding was over and we were securely committed to one another only increased after that. After the wedding, Paul returned to Washington for work for a couple of weeks while I packed up my life and prepared to move. During that two-week window, I spent as much time as I could with friends and family. A very large chapter in my life was coming to a close and a very new and different one was about to begin. Anyone with any little bit of empathy would have understood and given me some grace for those two weeks, knowing that he was going to have me the rest of his life once I moved. Unfortunately, Paul wasn't that person. He began to criticize me for not being available every time he called me or sent me a text message; it was all about him and his needs. There was no empathy or understanding for all that I was giving up.

All of the behaviors that I had attributed to our long-distance circumstances and his stressful job were about to get a whole lot worse and not better, as I'd imagined. Little irritations and frustrations were about to become major relational issues — and the happily ever after dream I thought I was entering was about to become a nightmare.

Chapter 13

HAPPILY EVER AFTER – NOT!

I was so excited to move to Washington. I couldn't wait to get there and start my new life; even the drive up was an adventure. In 2010, during the week of Thanksgiving, a major storm hit the Pacific Northwest. It snarled up roads something fierce in the Seattle area and delayed our drive by an entire day. It was so bad that when we drove into Yreka, just south of the California-Oregon border, the Highway Patrol was closing the onramp to northbound Interstate 5 because of ice along the Ashland Pass. Paul and I checked news and weather reports in our hotel room that night as he received firsthand accounts from his staff at Boeing Field in Seattle. "It's bad," they told us. We apparently were following the storm up the coast, and I silently thanked God for keeping us out of the worst of it. The next day dawned bright and clear and we easily made it over the pass. As we descended into Ashland, I was overcome with a newfound appreciation for our travel delay. In the dark and icy conditions the previous night, it must have been a nerve-wracking trek into Oregon for those drivers who attempted the crossing prior to the road closure.

The trip was an exciting one for me because I'd never traveled through that part of the country before. I'd never been further north than Mount Shasta, so everything after that was a new experience. The journey through Oregon was uneventful and we made good time until we encountered heavy traffic south of Portland. We were traveling the day before Thanksgiving and thought we might run into a mass exodus of workers heading home to start their holiday. We stopped for an early dinner, later discovered that road construction had caused the traffic delay, and then swung through Vancouver for a Starbucks fix a few hours later. At 9:30 p.m., we finally pulled up to Paul's home in Puyallup. Snow covered the lawn and ice had slicked up the driveway and sidewalk — thank goodness for the boots Paul bought me a couple of months earlier during one of his visits — me and all of my open-toed sandals wouldn't have survived very long in that weather.

We took in only the essentials that night, deciding to leave the unpacking for the next day. Paul opened the front door and as I stepped across the threshold to my new home, I got my first glimpse into the kind of home Paul kept when he wasn't trying to impress anyone. He had brought in several chairs belonging to a spare dining room set and left them sitting in the entry to the living room. Wedding gifts had arrived and they were opened and piled on the dining room chairs. A small desk in the foyer was littered with mail, notes, pens, and cell phone paraphernalia. And then there was the kitchen. The hi-top dining table was buried. More mail and pens had landed there, and had been joined by medications, dirty glasses and dishes, and other random household items. Jackets and security vests were draped over nearly every chair around the table. The kitchen sink and counters were filled with more dirty glasses and dishes. The refrigerator was full of miscellaneous leftovers and a good deal of long-forgotten food with expired dates. The only item that I knew to definitely be good was the enormous turkey sitting on one of the shelves. Paul and I had discussed Thanksgiving plans before he flew down to help me move, and I had asked him to buy a turkey before he left so that it would be defrosted by the time I arrived.

As I took in the sight, I thought to myself, *There is no way on God's green earth that I can prepare a Thanksgiving meal in this mess.* Just cleaning the kitchen would be a long day of work. I suggested that we postpone Thanksgiving dinner until Friday and steeled myself for whatever awaited me upstairs. Not surprisingly, things were kind of a wreck there, too. However, the master bedroom wasn't nearly the problem the kitchen had been. The master bath was going to need an overhaul, but that was going to be primarily an organizational project. I took a peek in the two spare bedrooms, one of which was being used as a den of sorts; again, it was going to be more of a tidying up task. The last bedroom, however, was like something out of the show "Hoarders". You could open the door but navigating through the room was challenging. There were plastic tubs all around the bed and each one had been filled to overflowing with papers, notebooks, pictures, books, memorabilia, Jeep parts, folders, pens, cards, and other miscellaneous items. The bed, which had no linens on it, was covered with more car parts, fishing rods, and stacks of mail. There was a crafting table on one side of the room and it, too, was covered. Even the closet was full. I would soon discover that every closet in the house was full.

I'd never known anyone who was as much of a packrat as Paul. He collected wrist watches and jackets. He had shoes and clothing that had never been worn. He still had uniforms and gear from his time in the Army 30 years earlier, along with old uniforms, jackets and vests from his years as a United Airlines maintenance employee. In the garage, Paul had boxes of emergency food rations, camping gear, broken doors and screens, old sets of tires, more fishing gear, and several standing tool cabinets filled to overflowing with every kind of tool known to man. He had buckets of miscellaneous nuts, bolts, and screws leftover from all of the projects he had worked on at the house. The man never threw anything out.

Now, some women might have taken one look at all that and run screaming from the house, never to return. I'll admit, I was a little overwhelmed after taking it all in, but one of my gifts is organization. Where others might have curled into a fetal position and called it a day, I was able to buckle down, roll up my sleeves, and get to work. We donated his living room furniture and replaced it with mine. We hung up my wall art and I stocked the kitchen with all of my appliances and gadgets. I scrubbed, scoured, and straightened things up. It took about a month, but I eventually reclaimed the house and turned it into a home.

Because of the timing of the move and Paul's work schedule, we had decided to postpone our honeymoon until the week between Christmas and New Year's. Our plans included a week in Long Beach, a small tourist community along the southwestern tip of Washington. I had been there once before, years earlier, and was anticipating a much more enjoyable experience with Paul. Unfortunately, because we'd never vacationed together before, and had never even talked about our expectations for the trip, I was sorely disappointed. I'm a morning person and I like to be up early to enjoy as much of the day as possible. I also like to walk. On vacation, I enjoy exploring the area on foot and window shopping. Paul, on the other hand, was used to starting his day closer to Noon and wasn't much of a walker. We never made it out for sightseeing until at least 1:00 in the afternoon. The weather that week wasn't conducive to sightseeing, so we spent a lot of time in the room. As honeymooners, you'd think that might have been ok, but my frustration just grew as the week progressed because Paul would end up napping every time he sat still for more than a few minutes. He wouldn't discover until long after we separated that he had significant health issues which had contributed to his fatigue during that time. By the end of the week, I had worked myself into a real lather about things. I felt like the entire week had been a waste of time and money, not exactly the report you want to get when asking about someone's honeymoon. I stewed in my juices the entire drive home and hardly said a word. We got home and unpacked in silence. It was New Year's Eve and as fireworks erupted around the neighborhood at midnight, fireworks were going off inside our home. I finally told Paul how I'd been feeling and let loose with all the tears that had been building up during our trip. While the honeymoon itself had been disappointing, the truth was that our relationship had suffered its first significant blow weeks earlier, and the Long Beach trip had only served to add insult to injury.

In December, as part of my work to reclaim Paul's house from neglect, we agreed that I would be in charge of household finances. In order to get my arms around things, I started asking him for information. I'd found various and sundry pieces of it in the mail that had been left on the dining room table, but there were still gaps. In some cases, I was able to call the service provider and get the information I needed, but some wouldn't release information because I wasn't yet named on the account. In the case of one of Paul's Jeeps, he couldn't put his hands on the loan documentation and payment coupons. That, in itself, was disturbing, but only slightly less than the fact that he had lied about the loan being paid off already. When confronted about it, he said, "Well, it's close to being paid off. There should only be a few more payments left." We never did find the paperwork, but that problem was solved when a repo man showed up at the house one day while Paul was at work. They weren't there because of a missed payment—though it turned out he *had* missed payments—they were there because Paul had canceled insurance on the Jeep, and you can't do that when the vehicle is being financed. Through the repo company, I was able to get the loan company's information, a copy of the loan document, and the remaining coupons. The Jeep was nowhere near paid off. There were still two years' of payments left to make on a loan that Paul had secured at a 25% interest rate. That's like buying a car with a credit card, and it gave me some insight into Paul's money management skills.

The Jeep, however, wasn't the only problem. One week, I noticed that our garbage hadn't been picked up. When I called the county, they gave me the standard line about not being able to give me any information because I wasn't named on the account. However, by asking a few properly worded questions, I was able to figure out that Paul had defaulted on the account and service had been suspended. When reviewing the electric and gas bills, I noticed extra fees had been tacked on and realized that those services had been disconnected and restarted in recent months, as well. Then there were the collection notices. Paul had been sent to collections, not because he had been hit with major, unexpected expenses, but because he was a procrastinator and didn't deal with things until forced into it. The collection bills were for *$15.00 each*, the amount of his insurance copayment. There was also a hospital bill for $200 that Paul claimed he didn't owe, but if he'd simply read the statement, he would have seen that the invoice was his share of cost after insurance covered the rest. That's how Paul was — he just ignored things until they became urgent, in-your-face issues that could no longer be ignored.

That's how I learned about "Sheila". I had noticed that the electric bill had both Paul and Sheila listed on it. Once again, when I called the service provider, they couldn't speak to me because I wasn't on the account. So I gave the bill to Paul and asked him to call the company, have her name removed, and have mine added.

After a week, I noticed that the bill was still sitting on the dash of his Jeep. After another week, I finally took back the bill and told Paul we were calling the company together. I had him put the company on speakerphone so I could verify that everything was resolved. On the call, they asked if Sheila was the ex-wife and Paul said she was. I thought it was odd that she was still on a utility bill since they had been divorced for nearly 10 years, but I let it go for the moment. I also thought it was odd that Paul had always referred to his ex-wife by a different name, possibly a nickname, but I also let that discrepancy go without comment. Later that same week, after clearing it with Paul, I started tackling the "hoarder" bedroom. In the first couple of boxes, I came across medical receipts and other documents that clearly indicated Sheila was a different woman from Paul's ex-wife. My internal radar was on high alert by this time, especially since all the paperwork had her listed with the same last name as Paul. *Good Lord*, I thought, *had he been married to her?* Paul had told me about only two women in his life — his ex-wife and a woman he had lived with for a few years — and neither of them had been named Sheila.

I called Paul at his office and told him what I'd found. I said, "Sheila isn't the same person as your ex-wife, is she?" After a long pause, he replied that no, she wasn't. That night, we had a little "coming to Jesus" talk. I asked him to tell me who Sheila was and how he knew her. He explained that he had met her several months before meeting me, and that she and her young daughter had moved in with him briefly while she got back on her feet. When asked about why she was using his last name, he told me it had just been easier to help her get medical services for her daughter. I asked him point blank, "Are you married to her?" Looking me straight in the eye, he replied, "No." I told him that lying was absolutely unacceptable to me and was a deal breaker in our marriage; there were a lot of things I was willing to tolerate, but lying wasn't one of them. I had been completely transparent with Paul about my own past and had expected the same of him. Understanding that we all have a past of some kind, I just wanted Paul to be honest about his so we could deal with it. I told him that if there was anything at all that he hadn't yet disclosed to me, that night was the time to do it. "You now know everything," he replied.

Later that week, as we continued to clean out that spare bedroom, I came across a marriage certificate to a woman named Luz. I showed it to Paul and he told me a story about how he had dated her briefly, and how she had been pressuring him to marry her so she could obtain her citizenship. He said she had forged his signature on this marriage license and that he'd met with an attorney to clear his name in the matter. Considering the rocky start to our own marriage, I kept the copy of the certificate—just in case.

Four months later, both Sheila and Luz would come back to haunt me.

As 2011 got underway, my marriage to Paul only deteriorated further. Communication was a huge problem for us, especially when it came to conflict resolution. Part of the problem was that I wanted to be the Holy Spirit in Paul's life; the other part was Paul's underdeveloped character.

Before meeting Paul, I'd never really had the chance to practice or prepare for being a godly wife. I hadn't prayed about it, and quite frankly, didn't really understand what it meant to be that kind of woman. In my first marriage, I'd been a parent. In my second marriage, I'd been a caregiver. In my marriage to Paul, I'd gone into things hoping and expecting to not have to be the leader in the relationship, but once I got up to Washington and saw the reality of Paul's life, I immediately moved back into both of my prior roles when it came to marriage — as parent *and* caregiver. I spent some time in prayer about it, but mostly I tried to control the situation and change Paul myself. I nagged, lectured, and explained. I pleaded, cried, and complained. Not surprisingly, nothing worked.

Paul, I discovered, had communication and conflict resolution skills that resembled a child's more than an adult's. Anytime Paul didn't get his way, he would pout and sulk. If I exercised any kind of personal boundary or stood up to him in any way, he would imply that I didn't love him. He just couldn't understand why I wouldn't go along with him and his way of doing things all the time. Paul wanted what he wanted, and he didn't understand how his actions affected others, especially me. He regularly exhibited selfish, impatient, and blame-shifting behaviors.

One source of constant conflict was money. Paul made great money working for Boeing and he was used to having lots of disposable income. However, once he married me and assumed all of my monthly credit card payments, that disposable income was drastically reduced. It also didn't help that I had organized the budget and made sure we paid all of the household bills — and paid them on time. Paul had never lived on a budget. He had gotten away with it because of all the money he made. When a creditor would come knocking and asking about late payments, he always had enough money to just write a check and bring the account current. Once I started holding his feet to the fire, though, he began to rebel. One of the things I asked Paul to do was notify me *before* he used his debit card. It wasn't uncommon for me to check our balance and find several surprise transactions, making it nearly impossible for me to manage the checking account and plan for the things we needed. I also had a conversation with Paul about the grocery budget. I told him we could afford to pack his lunches *or* he could have an allowance to go out and eat every day, but we couldn't do both. He opted to take his lunch and I packed him one each day. Imagine my surprise, then, to find debit transactions at restaurants when I checked the bank account. Months later, in counseling, Paul would tell me that I hadn't been packing enough food in his lunch. That didn't hold much water, though, since I had repeatedly asked him about his lunches when I discovered the restaurant charges, and there had been ample opportunity for him to say something. Paul simply wasn't able or willing to make a decision and remain accountable to it. He wanted to live according to his whims and not be responsible to anyone or anything.

Adopting Shasta really brought this behavior to light. Paul had been suggesting for a while that we get a dog. I knew it was too early in our relationship to add the responsibility for a pet but Paul was insistent; he wanted me to have a companion since he was at work so much, but couching it as a supposed benefit for me wasn't really working. I had no problem being alone during the day, and I knew that because of Paul's long hours, I would get stuck with the lion's share of responsibility for the dog. On top of that, our backyard wasn't dog-friendly. Paul's packrat tendencies carried over into the yard and there were several items that needed to go to the dump, including old storage bins. Additionally, there were low spots along the fence line, loose boards in the fence itself, and a gate in serious need of repair. Last but not least, the yard simply needed maintenance. If you're going to have a dog pooping in the yard, it's far easier to clean up if the lawn is kept short. I kept telling Paul that if he wanted a dog, all of those issues needed to be addressed. Over and over, he promised to deal with them but nothing ever happened.

One weekend, Paul drove me to the local animal shelter as a surprise. We took a look around and picked out a dog. We had to wait a couple of days for some paperwork to clear, and during that time I decided against the adoption. Another couple of weeks went by and Paul wanted to visit yet another shelter. I was getting tired of constantly being the "bad cop" in our relationship and I relented for good the second time. Despite our landlord's request that we adopt a small breed, Paul chose a Labrador and German Shepherd mix. Amazingly, the landlord approved the adoption.

It wasn't but one week after the adoption that our first conflict arose. Paul called me one evening from work and asked me to drive out and meet him for dinner; it was something we'd enjoyed doing once or twice a week since Paul was at work almost every day and it gave us a little more time together. We'd only had the dog about a week and she was still getting used to her new surroundings; I wasn't comfortable leaving her alone in the Jeep while we ate. I told Paul as much and asked for a raincheck on dinner. He wasn't understanding about it at all, and began to whine and complain that the dog was more important than him.

Against my better judgment, I relented. As expected, Shasta wasn't happy about being abandoned in the car—this was a shelter dog, remember—and I knew it wasn't going to end well. After dinner, Paul walked me out to the Jeep where we discovered Shasta had chewed up the gear shifter. Paul wasn't happy about that at all. I wanted to yell at him, "Well, what did you expect?! I told you this was a bad idea!" Miraculously, I managed to keep my mouth shut, but I'm certain my body language conveyed the message all the same.

Paul and I had radically different ideas regarding pet ownership. He wanted the dog but didn't want to invest time or money into her. He only wanted to deal with her when it was fun or convenient and I was left to handle all the hard stuff. I ended up taking care of all the yard maintenance and cleaning up after the dog. I took her to all the vet appointments and administered all the medications. I took her to all the training classes and spent time during the day keeping her entertained. Paul got what he wanted, and my life just got more complicated and challenging. That, unfortunately, would be a recurring theme throughout the remainder of our marriage.

Chapter 14

THE BIG REVEAL

The longer I lived with Paul, the more I realized that the man he had portrayed himself to be during dating looked nothing like the man I had married. But the truth was that he *was* the same man; I had just chosen to ignore the warning signs. For example, it should have been a huge red flag that Paul didn't invite any of his friends to our wedding. He also didn't ask one of his own friends to be his best man. People who are Christ-followers have godly, healthy relationships in their life, and Paul's lack of that in his own life should have had me putting on the brakes. I also hadn't taken the time to observe Paul in a variety of life circumstances and confirm that he was walking the talk. I took Paul at his word in everything. He told me he was debt-free and I believed him. He told me he was a Christian but I didn't wait to see what kind of fruit his connection with God was producing; that particular discrepancy was the most disappointing of all.

When I got to Washington, I assumed Paul and I would attend church together every weekend. Part of my desire for a godly husband was to share my passion for Christ with someone every day. I wanted to pursue God with my husband, serve with him, worship with him, pray with him, and study with him. With Paul, those things never materialized. If I had never prodded him, he never would have gone to church with me. He used to read his Bible pretty regularly, but his life didn't demonstrate that he was applying the things he read. He was going through the motions but not really investing himself in his relationship with Jesus. We only prayed together when I asked about it, and I rarely saw Paul take the time to spend quiet time alone in devotions or journaling. He sometimes said he spent that time while driving to and from work, but again, I didn't see evidence of that in how he lived his life and made decisions, or in how he treated me.

One night, when Paul got home from work, he complained that I was always reading my Bible and journaling. I almost always got up before Paul, and

I would head downstairs to the kitchen to read my Bible and journal until he joined me for a late breakfast. In the evenings, I would do the same thing until he got home, which was usually near midnight. So while it's true that Paul usually found me with my nose buried in reading and journaling, when he joined me downstairs or came home, I wrapped up my reading and focused on him. His complaint both surprised and disturbed me. I assumed Paul would love that his wife was investing time in her relationship with Christ; any God-fearing husband *would* find that quality endearing and admirable in his partner. Proverbs 31:10 says that an excellent wife is hard to find and is more valuable than precious jewels. The fact that Paul was upset with me for trying to be that kind of woman led me to question his own spiritual condition. *Was Paul really a believer at all*, I wondered? *Or, had he just been giving lip service to me – and to God – all this time?*

I once heard a pastor say, "If you want to know how a man is leading in his marriage, take a look at his wife. Is she thriving and growing under his care and leadership, or is she shriveling up and dying?" It was about this time, in the spring of 2011, when I started to realize that I was withering up on the inside. My passion and fire for Jesus felt like they were slowly being extinguished in the marriage. I was still attending the foursquare church near our home every weekend, and I had joined a women's group that met every Monday, but the lack of leadership at home was taking its toll. I felt like I was swimming upstream against a heavy current of opposition. Despite Paul's criticism, my daily reading and journaling were keeping me afloat, and one entry in particular strengthened my desire to persevere. In Psalm 89:30-35, God talks about how He will discipline His people when they disobey Him, but He will never stop loving them, never stop being faithful, and He will never go back on His promises.

When I started to question Paul's relationship with Christ, I began to wonder and worry about my own status with God. I thought that I might be guilty by association, and that God would punish me right along with Paul. It certainly felt like I was being punished because our marriage wasn't improving despite all of the various efforts I was making. But in reading Psalm 89, I realized that if God disciplines those who ignore His statutes, He also honors those who *do* obey Him. I needed to mind my own relationship with God, regardless of what Paul did or didn't do. I needed to go to church, with or without Paul. I needed to attend my women's group, whether or not Paul ever joined a men's group. I needed to continue reading my Bible and journaling, even if Paul didn't set aside quiet time for himself. And I needed to apply God's Word to my daily life, no matter what Paul thought or said. God drove the point home in another piece of Scripture from that day's reading in John 21. In verses 21 and 22, Jesus rebukes Peter when he questions Him about the fate of another disciple, and basically tells him it's none of his business with three little words, "You, follow Me!"

And follow Him I would, right into a devastating revelation just a few weeks later.

I was in the garage searching for a tire pump when it happened.

Paul told me he had a tire pump for the bicycles, but I couldn't find it anywhere. I finally thought to check the tool cabinets. The bottom drawer in each of them was large enough to house a tire pump, and wasn't it sort of a tool, anyway? I opened the drawer in the first one and found nothing. I opened the drawer in the second cabinet and found… manila file folders. I started to question why on earth file folders would be in a tool cabinet, and then reminded myself that this was Paul we were talking about; I was likely to find anything, anywhere. I grabbed the stack of folders and pulled them out, immediately displacing a sheaf of papers all over the garage floor. *Great*, I thought, *just what I need, another mess to clean up.* I retrieved the papers and turned them over to place back in the top folder, and that's when I saw it.

Staring me in the face, in black and white, was a marriage certificate—*for Paul and Sheila.* I'm not sure how long I stood there, frozen, while I looked over every detail of that paper. It was Paul's name. It was Paul's address. It was Paul's signature. It was all the same information he had provided on our own marriage license and it was dated March 10, 2010—less than four months before we had been matched on eHarmony.

I walked back into the house still clutching the papers, barely aware of what I was doing, though I recall telling myself to breathe. I actually said it out loud. "Breathe. Just breathe." I sat down at the kitchen table and tried to make some sense of what I had in my hands. First and foremost, Paul had lied to me back in December when I'd first learned about Sheila and asked him point blank if they were married. Worse than that, he had been deceiving me from the very beginning of our relationship. He hadn't even mentioned her as a dating relationship, let alone as a marriage. *What else had he lied about?* I wondered. As I sat there, a new and crushing possibility took shape. *What if he was still married to her? What if my marriage to Paul wasn't valid?*

In that moment, everything I thought I knew about myself and about Paul came crashing down around me. The life I'd been living for five months was just an illusion. It had been based upon a lie, and quite possibly, far more than just one. I had given up everything to move to Washington—and I'd done it for *a lie.* Just then, the phone rang. I checked the caller ID; it was Paul. He was the first, and last, person I wanted to speak to right then. We'd already had several disagreements about me not always answering his calls. Paul honestly believed I should literally be at his beck and call, and got upset when I didn't answer or call back right away. I thought about letting the call go to voice mail, and then decided I didn't need the grief. I pressed the answer button, "Hello?" "Hey, how're you doing?" came his trademark reply. "I've been better," I told him, and he immediately wanted to know what was wrong. I told him I didn't want to get into it right then, but he persisted. Paul really didn't know how to take no for an answer. *Fine,* I thought, *you want to talk, let's talk.*

I told him I'd found the marriage certificate for him and Sheila and that we had some major issues to deal with when he got home that night. I lit into him about how we might not be legally married, and how on earth could he have lied to me about such an important detail in his life? I reminded him of all the times he had professed his faith and how he was adamant that we not invite sin into our relationship, and how hypocritical it was considering that he had been lying from the start. I wanted to know if he had ever filed for divorce from Sheila. I wanted to know all the other things I didn't know. Most of all, though, I think I just wanted to know *why* he had lied in the first place.

Isn't that what we always want to know? When we've been hurt and wronged by someone, especially a loved one, we always want to know why they did it. We think somehow that our understanding will lessen our pain, but it never does. Betrayal is an injury to the heart, not the intellect. An understanding of the perpetrator's motives can help us make sense of the hurt, but it doesn't really heal the heart. Though, as in my case, understanding can be incorrectly used to bring about a false sense of healing and restoration. I believed that as my understanding of Paul's reasons grew, so did healing between us. I believed I could think my way into reconciliation but my heart knew better. Things would start to improve on the surface, but then my heart would drag us back down. My heart, and not my head, was in the driver's seat and it was quick to remind me that it wouldn't be ignored.

After my rant on the phone, Paul was understandably reluctant to come home and face me. He called me a bit later in the afternoon and asked if he should come home. I thought, *You're a grown man. Figure it out yourself!* I told him it was his decision but I knew he and his staff had a plane to test in eastern Washington, and he was scheduled to fly out the next morning. My lack of boundaries kicked in. I told him he should come home and pack for the trip, and that he couldn't just blow off work, but the truth was that he could have, and should have. After God, I was supposed to be his priority, even before work. He had just been informed that a foolish decision on his part had critically injured his marriage of five months. He should have blown off everything else and come home to start the healing process. Instead, Paul was most concerned with himself. He was worried about facing the consequences of his actions. He was worried that I might leave him while he was away on his trip, and that he would come home to an empty house.

Paul walked into the house just a few minutes after we ended the call. He had let me believe that he was still at Boeing Field when he called; in reality he had been sitting in his Jeep, parked in front of our house. He had been home even while asking me if he should come home. *Unbelievable!* I thought. Everything about Paul stemmed from deception; it was like he had absolutely no concept of authenticity or integrity. He walked over to me, not in humility or remorse, but rather like a little kid who's just gotten caught with his hand in the cookie jar, hoping that you'll find him cute enough to forgive and excuse. I still remember the slight smile on his face, like he was just embarrassed instead of ashamed, as if what he had done wasn't that big of a deal. I reached out and grabbed the front of his shirt. "You shit," I whispered. Knowing that I never swore, Paul must have thought that was the extent of my rebuke because he visibly relaxed at that moment, and even let out a small laugh. He took my hand. "C'mon, let's go to dinner," he said. In shock, and unable to fully grasp the enormity of what had happened that afternoon, I went along.

Chapter 15

"YOU NEED TO LEAVE, TODAY!"

In the weeks following the discovery of the marriage certificate, my shock began to wear off and anger began to set in. In that anger, I started demanding answers and accountability. For starters, I wanted to know what had really happened between him and Sheila. He told me he had met her online in the wake of his long-term, live-in relationship dissolving. Soon after, he invited her to move in with him. They had quickly married, and just as quickly she had decided to leave. I discovered that Paul's habit was to immediately seek out new dating relationships as his preferred method for coping with loss in his life. That's how he met Sheila, and that's how he met me. It was also how he had met and married Luz. She hadn't forged his signature on the marriage certificate I had found. He had dated her briefly and then married her, and it wasn't to gain her citizenship. He had simply been on the rebound from his first marriage.

According to Paul, Sheila told him she would file the papers for divorce — which she never did — and he never thought to go back and make sure the marriage had been dissolved. When asked why he didn't disclose the relationship to me, he just said he was embarrassed by his poor decision making in the matter and didn't want to bring it up. All of it sounded so lame to me. I just couldn't figure out how someone got to be 60 years old with such a lack of coping and life management skills. I honestly didn't know how he held down a job. All I could come up with was that he really loved his work, and we have a tendency to apply ourselves to the things we genuinely enjoy. Everything else, though, has a tendency to suffer; that was certainly true for Paul. One of the things I found as I was cleaning out the spare bedroom was a report card for Paul from the third grade. His teacher had written that while Paul was smart, he was also lazy. He didn't apply himself and his poor grades were a result of nothing more than carelessness about homework and other assignments. I thought to myself, *Nothing much has changed in 50 years.* I could have written the same comments about Paul and the way he was living life with me.

Paul was anything but dumb. You don't get to work as a maintenance crew chief on passenger jets if you're stupid, but everything outside of his work suffered terribly. Paul invested himself so heavily into his job that there wasn't time or energy left for anyone or anything else. His home, his finances, and his relationships were dealt with only when they became dire emergencies and he was forced to reckon with them. If they required more than a quick fix, he didn't know how to persevere through the process and achieve resolution.

Now that his marriage to Sheila was out in the open, Paul just wanted to move on with life but my heart wouldn't let me do that. I needed to work back through the hurt and deal with the underlying issues before I could move forward. Every time I tried to have a conversation about what had happened, Paul accused me of being unforgiving and unloving. "If you really loved me," he said, "you would just let it go and move on." His accusations, on top of his betrayal, were more than I could take. We needed professional help. I suggested we visit our pastor, who then recommended a marriage counselor.

As Paul told the counselor what had happened, and got to the part about not dissolving the marriage and not disclosing it to me, he looked at me and then back at Paul and said, "Oops." That, I mused, was the understatement of the century. The counselor then told us he wanted to meet again the following week, and basically told Paul that I was to be calling the shots for the moment. I had been betrayed and my feelings took precedence. Whatever I needed to process, I was to be given the grace and the space in which to do it, for as long as I needed to do it.

One night during that week, I was feeling especially vulnerable and broken. I was in a quiet mood and really didn't want to discuss much of anything with Paul. He had asked me to tell him when I was feeling out of sorts so that he wouldn't be blindsided by my mood changes. I didn't think that was unreasonable and I agreed. That night, I called Paul at work to give him a heads up regarding my mood. He seemed fine with it until he got home a few hours later. I was in bed reading when he came in. Paul walked into the bedroom and announced he was moving out. I took a deep breath and called to mind a verse I had studied earlier that day: Exodus 14:14 says that God will fight for you, you need only to be still. If there was about to be a battle, I needed God out in front of me.

I calmly replied, "OK. I understand if that's something you need to do right now." Paul stood there for a minute rocking back and forth on his feet, and I could sense that both barrels of the gun were being loaded. A few seconds later, he began to lay into me. He told me I was cold-hearted. He accused me of giving up on the marriage. He said I wasn't behaving like a God-fearing, Christian woman. I sat there, incredulous, as I listened to the litany of insults and accusations. Here I was, the one who had been betrayed, and I was being made out as the bad guy. He once again stated he couldn't stay in the house and was moving out. I again told him I understood, which prompted him to remove his wedding ring and toss it to me, saying he didn't need it anymore. He unleashed another stream of accusations while I sat there thinking, *Lord, if you're going to fight for me, now would be a really great time for You to step in.* Paul finished his tirade by telling me that there was no point in continuing the counseling sessions and he wouldn't be attending with me any longer.

Paul was upset with me for having done exactly what he asked. I gave him a heads up that I wasn't in a good mood and to not expect much from me that night. He was also upset with me when I agreed with everything he threatened in his rant. That, my friends, is called emotional manipulation. It's like when a child says they're going to run away. They announce everything they're doing along the way: "I'm running away!", "I'm packing up my stuff now!", "I'm heading out the door!", "I'm really leaving now!", "You're going to be sorry once I'm gone!" Each time you go along with what they say, they make another statement instead of actually leaving. The threat is their way of getting attention and keeping you engaged. When you respond in a calm and reasonable manner, it just upsets them and they look for ways to prolong the emotional game. Every time I agreed with Paul, it just frustrated him because what he really wanted was my time and attention, even if it was in the form of a pointless argument. I'd been playing that game with Paul the whole time we'd been together and I was physically and emotionally exhausted; I was done and I didn't feel like playing anymore. Paul was losing his playmate, and out of fear he lashed out. As I mentioned earlier, understanding Paul's behavior helped me to make sense of things, but it did little to actually foster healing. In order for that to happen, I needed Paul to take responsibility for his actions and start changing his behavior instead of just giving lip service to it.

When we returned to the counselor's office a week later, I told him about that night. The counselor just looked at Paul as if to say, "Dude, really? Did you not hear anything I told you last week?" Paul apologized then, but over the next two or three visits nothing much changed; we just covered the same territory over and over again. I desperately needed a break from the tension and stress — and God was about to give me one.

In the two months after finding the marriage certificate, things hadn't improved; in fact, they'd gotten worse. The constant tension from Paul wanting to move forward and me needing to work back into our issues was tearing at my sanity. Patience was nearly non-existent for me and any little strain sent me into a crying jag. Paul's lack of understanding and constant attacking weren't helping and I never hesitated to tell him so. When I moved to Washington, I hadn't bothered getting a job because Paul had told me his income was enough to support us both. He didn't want me to work and I was looking forward to being a housewife and homemaker. That became a huge problem when things fell apart in our marriage because I had no resources to move out into a place of my own. I was stuck in the house with Paul and that just added to my stress level. I'd reached my breaking point and needed God to do something.

In early June, I finally reached the end of my own rope and resources. Paul had gone to work and I was sitting at the kitchen table working through my daily Bible reading. Proverbs 24:16 had come up twice in my devotionals that morning and I made the following entry in my journal: *Proverbs 24:16 is in front of me twice today. My email devotional included it when talking about how failure isn't final. Failure is often a bridge to God's blessing. A righteous man rises every time he stumbles. This situation (my broken marriage) isn't an end unto itself. It's just a bridge to greater intimacy with God and a transition to something better... Reveal a direction for me... where does the bridge lead and what is my next step?* The weight of the previous year and the gravity of my mistakes had taken their toll. I'd wandered far from God in pursuing Paul and now I was like the prodigal son in the pigpen, realizing how low I'd been allowed to fall. I'd lived life on my terms for the past year and felt broken beyond repair. I knew I had no right to ask God for anything in that moment, even forgiveness, yet that's exactly what I did.

I began to cry as I confessed a year's worth of rebellion and foolishness. I had rushed into things and hadn't waited on God. I had leaned on my own understanding. I had chased after what I wanted, the consequences be damned. When things had fallen apart, I'd tried to fix them in my own power and had succeeded in only digging myself into a deeper pit.

My self-sufficiency was exhausted and I needed a Savior. I begged God for a breakthrough: "Start to improve our marriage, or open a door for me to leave," I pleaded. I committed to wait on God and not make a move until I heard clearly from Him.

As the week progressed, I had several conversations with my former pastor and a few close friends who knew what had happened. Over two consecutive days, I spoke with four different people and each of them asked me the same question, almost verbatim: Is it possible that Paul's pre-existing marriage to Sheila is God's way of giving you an out from *your* marriage? It was awfully coincidental that I would be asked the exact same thing by four different people in such a short span of time. *Ok Lord*, I thought, *if You are giving me an out, then open a door for me and I'll walk through.* I figured I could take a baby step in that direction by planning a visit back to Folsom for a couple of weeks to clear my head and get some rest before making any major decisions. I made plans to meet up with the friends who had stood up for me and Paul at our wedding; they were going to be in Portland later in June and I figured I could drive back down to California with them.

When I told Paul about my plans, it didn't come as much of a surprise when he started making it all about him. He was upset that I'd told other people about our situation. Considering how secretive he'd been with me, it was only natural that he'd want to keep the details from others. He didn't understand my need for a support system and felt like I'd betrayed his trust. Quite frankly, I really didn't care about how my behavior was impacting Paul at that point. My main concern was my own well-being and getting out of his presence for a while. While we were arguing about all of that, he asked me how soon I could be packed up and out of the house. I guess he figured since I wanted a break, I could just get out of the house permanently. I just looked at him for a minute, wondering when this had become my life. "I don't know," I replied, "but I'll start packing this afternoon and work on finding another place to stay." It was just more manipulation — evidenced by the fact that he immediately backpedaled from his request when I agreed to it — nevertheless, I packed a suitcase in preparation.

That night, when Paul got home from work, he lit into me yet again about how cold I was to be leaving him and talking with others about our marriage. I was the one in the wrong, and I wasn't behaving like a Christian woman. *Great, here we go again*, I thought. Then, he tossed out the one piece of Scripture he had at his disposal. "You know," he said, "God hates divorce."

"That's true," I replied, "but last time I checked, God also hated lying, deceiving, and committing adultery." "I didn't cheat on you!" he shot back. Now, it was late, and I didn't want to have a debate about what constituted adultery; yet there I stood in our bedroom, trying to explain to Paul how he had made me the "other woman" because he was still married to Sheila. True, he hadn't cheated on me, but he had still led us into an adulterous scenario. In all the conversations we had, he never understood or accepted that fact. At 4 a.m., we finally called it a night.

After a short but deep sleep, I was awake at 9:00. Paul remained sound asleep while I showered and got ready for the day. As I stood in front of the mirror putting on my makeup, God spoke to me so suddenly and clearly in my head that it was nearly audible. "You need to leave *today*." The statement was accompanied by a physical pressure, like someone or something exerting force or authority around me. Even as I kept hearing the statement in my head, I started to mentally argue with God. *But, I'm not ready to go yet. I'm not supposed to meet my friends for another week and a half. This isn't part of the plan,* I thought. And then, the dumbest reason of all popped into my head. *Who's going to take care of the dog?* I wondered. Immediately, I heard in my head, "I'll take care of the dog. You need to go, today!"

By this time, my heart was pounding in my ears and I felt like I was watching someone else move around the house. I finished my makeup and hair, and then packed my toiletries bag. My suitcase, coincidentally, was already packed and ready to go; funny how God orchestrates those things. I packed a tote box with books and journals and went downstairs to move money from the joint savings account into my individual checking account. I had brought $3,000 with me into the marriage and that's exactly what I moved into my account. I set my luggage and tote box next to the front door and returned upstairs to tell Paul about my change in plans, including the transfer of funds. I still expected to be gone only about two weeks, and to resume counseling when I got back. I told Paul I just needed a break from things to clear my head and get some rest. He was, as you might guess, very upset about the change. The fact that I had transferred funds was a sign to him that I wasn't planning on returning. I told him the fact that I was leaving all of my belongings at the house was a sign that I *was* going to be back. Nevertheless, he asked me to leave my joint debit card with him, along with my house key. I was too emotionally frazzled to put up a fight and I left both items on the kitchen table before I left.

After saying goodbye to Shasta and Paul, I walked out of the house and got into my car. I must have sat there for almost two minutes just trying to re-engage with reality. Everything felt so surreal. I hadn't been prepared to leave that day and I didn't have a plan. I was completely at the mercy and direction of God.

"OK Lord," I whispered, "now what?" and started the engine.

Chapter 16

THE PRODIGAL RETURNS

On June 16, 2011, I left the house I'd worked so hard to make into a home for me and Paul. I left with the intention of returning in a few weeks, but it would be eight months before I'd walk through that front door again.

It's funny the things we cling to as anchors or touch points in our life. God, obviously, was the first and foremost anchor for me, but Starbucks was a close second at that time in my life. Aside from the house, it was the place where I spent most of my time. Paul and I had gone there every day before he left for work, and my women's group met at a local Starbucks as well. I figured it was as good a place as any to stop and listen for God's next direction. As I sat there with my coffee and checked my phone, I read through that day's devotional email and got my first bit of confirmation that I was doing the right thing.

I don't recall the verse, but the topic was leaving the disobedient people in our life to God and His care. The author gave examples of such people, and some of the phrases she used perfectly described Paul's attitude and some of the things that had come out of his mouth in recent months. It was like God saying, "There's no more for you to do with Paul. Leave him to Me now." I finished the devotional then suddenly remembered I had scheduled a coffee date with my women's group leader that afternoon. It would put me on the road late in the afternoon, but I decided to keep the appointment.

Meeting with "Mary" turned out to be an incredible godsend. I told her all that had happened in recent weeks and that I was now on the road back to Folsom to take a break from Paul. She asked if I had removed my name from the utilities and other shared accounts as a way of protecting my credit. Of course I hadn't, but it seemed like the wise thing to do once she mentioned it. Mary and I then looked up all of the phone numbers I needed and we made the calls. When we finished, she took me next door and helped me open a post office box and submit a change of address for my mail. She kept one of the keys and told me she would check the box each week and send me anything of importance. I didn't know I was going to need Mary's help that day, but God saw all of this coming and He had prepared for it. Even though I hadn't planned on leaving that day, God had orchestrated everything I would need, including a little help from my friends.

Once I got on the road, I called the friends I had planned to meet in Portland to let them know I was heading home that day. I didn't go into details, but simply told them that God had opened a door and I'd had to leave sooner than expected. They immediately went into help mode. As it turned out, that Thursday was my friend's husband's day off work. He was instrumental in finding me a place to stay overnight in Portland and arranging a flight for my friend so she could meet me there early the next morning. They had decided I shouldn't drive all the way back to Folsom alone, so she was coming up to keep me company. Knowing what lay ahead, God had placed these friends in my life months earlier during the wedding plans and positioned them to be my life raft when I needed it.

There was, however, one particular prompting that I ignored and it would become a huge sticking point during the time I was separated from Paul. As I left my meeting with Mary and was still just a couple of miles away from my house, I realized I hadn't taken the boxes with my personal and financial records. I had left behind tax records, automobile records, banking and payroll information, and other business paperwork. I felt like God was prompting me to go back to the house and get it, but I didn't want to face Paul again. I was already on the road and didn't want to backtrack and delay my trip any longer. It was a bad move on my part because Paul would eventually use that as leverage against me. If I'd had those records with me, I could easily have walked away when Paul refused my request to come back and get my things later on. Because I'd left my house key, I had surrendered any and all access to the house. It was a decision I regretted for many months following my departure, and was the source of countless hours of frustration. God would later redeem that mistake and get me back into the house in a way that only He could, but it was an important lesson for me in learning to trust God and obey Him even when it was the last thing I felt like doing.

When I got to Portland and checked into the hotel, I was beyond ready for a night of rest. The constant tension and stress had left me unable to think clearly. Paul, however, wasn't ready to let go. He called and sent text messages that evening, some to simply inquire how I was doing while others were full of accusations about me having gone to Portland to meet up with an imaginary boyfriend. *This*, I thought, *is why I needed the break in the first place*. I finally told Paul that I would be out of pocket until I got to Folsom. Once I arrived, I would let him know I'd made it safely. Until then, I needed a communications blackout.

The next morning, I picked up my friend at the Portland airport and we made it back to Folsom that evening. Despite my request to not communicate, I received several voice mail messages and text messages from Paul during our drive back. I replied with one, brief text message to let him know I'd arrived in Folsom and would be in touch after a few days. That night, for the first time in many months, I slept well. No late night arguments. No lying in bed next to Paul, both of us wide awake and tense, wondering if we were moments away from another debate. No leaving the bedroom abruptly to go sleep in a different room. There was just silence and peace. I can still remember waking up the following morning, on a Saturday, and looking out the window to the backyard. It was a beautiful day, bright and clear. As I laid there listening to the neighborhood waking up, I realized I felt *safe*. For months, I'd endured verbal abuse, emotional blackmail, and various forms of manipulation. Over time, it had become normal under the circumstances. I didn't realize how unsafe I'd felt in those conditions until that first morning back in Folsom.

When I'd gotten on the road two days earlier, I sent my pastor a text message telling him I'd left Paul and was on my way back to Folsom. His text message back read, "I'm proud of you." At the time, I didn't feel like I'd done anything worthy of pride. I'd made a huge mistake going up to Washington in the first place, and now I was coming back just seven months later in the wake of incredible deception. My pastor knew all that, and I'm certain he understood the battle which had been raging within me. He would have known the conflict in my heart as I battled between staying in a marriage I'd desperately wanted and leaving an incredibly unhealthy situation. I had asked God for guidance and He had opened a door. I had taken a huge leap of faith and followed Him away from Paul back into the waiting arms of people who knew and loved me, and would be there to help me heal—and that had taken courage.

God's natural bent is to deliver us into His best. Our natural bent is towards all lesser things. Any time we break from our default condition to follow God into His will, it's something we can be proud of.

Luke 15:20 is my favorite verse in the Bible. It is a perfect picture of the heart of God towards each one of us. Whether we are coming to Him for the first time, or returning to Him for the hundredth time, this verse from the story of the prodigal son beautifully illustrates how God responds the moment we begin to move towards Him. He doesn't wait until we've cleaned up our act and He doesn't make us return all the way to Him. God tells us that while we are still a long way off, He sees us and starts running to meet us, and He does so in order to scoop us up and welcome us into His loving arms.

The night I spent in Portland, I had a prodigal son moment like that. I was in the shower and suddenly I was filled with the truth that I was a daughter of the King, and that my value and worth were rooted in that identity. It filled every part of me—physically, mentally, and emotionally—and I remember just stopping in the shower and sobbing for a while. It was like the embrace that the prodigal son and his father shared, both of them crying while they rejoiced at being reunited. In following my own desires and running off to Washington, I had wandered and squandered just like the prodigal son, but God hadn't written me

211

off. Instead, He had been watching and waiting for my return. In Portland, I had taken only the first step but that was enough for God. I had demonstrated obedience in waiting for Him to make it clear that He was opening a door for me to return to Folsom. Afterward, when He spoke and commanded me to leave, I left even though it wasn't in my timing. I had taken just a couple of small steps towards Him, like an infant taking those first tentative steps when learning to walk, then my heavenly Dad was there to take hold of me in His sure and protective grip.

I think we can mistakenly read the story of the prodigal son and believe that those moments will be few and far between in our life. We might see ourselves as the prodigal only when we stumble in significant ways, but I learned something in the years after I returned to California: We don't have prodigal moments or seasons; we live prodigal lives. Every day, we wander and squander. We go to work and we get caught up in problems and challenges, and don't give God a passing thought for hours at a stretch. We go to school and dive into the culture of what's cool and what's not, and forget all that God has told us about what really matters. We can even go to church and seek to learn in our own understanding, and serve in our own power, and forget that God's Spirit lives within us to do those things. We wander and squander all throughout our days, but God is constantly there to receive us back into His embrace. He never stops being our Dad no matter how many times we wander away. He never refuses us when we return to Him. The robe, the ring, and the sandals are never withheld from us.

While returning to God was certainly the biggest and most important piece of my return to Folsom, it wasn't the only one. There were practical considerations and those were trickier things to navigate. Leaving Folsom had been a very public thing. I had been established at both work and church, and both of those communities sent me off with a measure of fanfare. There had been a going away celebration at the office with parting gifts, a picture slideshow, and a presentation from my staff. At church, my pastor had called me up on stage and presented me with a thank you gift for my service there and prayed for the next season in my life. I'd left Folsom amid cheers and tears, and now I was back just seven months later, tail between my legs—humbled, humiliated and broken. Only about five people knew what had happened and that I was back in town, and I was quite content to keep it that way for a few days. I needed some time to simply catch my breath and rest, and to get my head wrapped around my current circumstances.

For the first time in my life, at the age of 46, I was without a home, a job, and possessions. I had packed my car with one suitcase of clothing, a toiletries bag, and a box full of books and journals. Everything else which had defined my life had been left in Washington. In one fell swoop, I'd been stripped of everything that had given me a sense of identity and meaning. I was no longer the owner of stuff. I was no longer a renter. I was no longer an employee. I was no longer a wife. I was no longer a ministry leader. Even my perceptions about myself had been shattered. I'd always considered myself a good, solid Christian but that illusion had come crashing down in Washington. I'd always thought of myself as being pretty wise and discerning, but my experiences with Paul had revealed my blind and foolish nature. I'd always prided myself on being independent and self-sufficient, but now I was without resources and totally dependent upon the grace of God and the kindness of my friends and family.

In pursuing a relationship with Paul, I'd been busy with a lot of striving, both physically and mentally. I'd made things happen in my own power and through my own efforts. In the aftermath of it all coming apart, there was nothing I could do for myself to fix the situation and there was no pulling myself up by my bootstraps. I was forced to do what Psalm 46:10 so wisely advises: I had to be still and know that God was everything He always claimed to be. In fact, it would be about 2 ½ years of stillness—literally and figuratively—as I experienced the depth and breadth of His love and grace.

Chapter 17

IN THE VALLEY OF THE SHADOW

I have learnt to love the darkness of sorrow; there you can see the brightness of His face.
– Madame Guyon

He did not hide deep darkness from my face.
– Job 23:17

In October, just 3 ½ months after returning to Folsom, I decided it was time to move out of my friends' home and into my own apartment. I'd been rehired by my former employer and was bringing in a regular paycheck once again, and I'd recently started counseling through a Soul Care program at a nearby church. Having a place of my own where I could process through the things we discussed would be an important part of my healing.

Compared to the apartment I'd had in Folsom, the place I rented in Rocklin was depressing and dreary. Grey carpet and poor lighting made it feel like a prison; it also didn't help that my apartment had an insect problem due to my apartment being located in a building that backed up to a greenbelt. During my first couple of months there, I dreaded coming home because I knew there would be some kind of bug hunting I'd have to do. It was bad enough having to fight with Paul, but having to fight with the lease managers to get the bug issue fixed just added to my tension and stress.

As I settled in to the apartment, I also settled in to the reality of my situation. Nothing in my life at this time was as good or nice as it had been in Folsom. I wasn't in a job that suited my gifting and abilities. I wasn't in a home where I felt safe and comfortable. I didn't have any of my own possessions or mementos. I wasn't making as much money as before because, after marrying Paul, I'd lost supplemental income from a prior marriage. Every day was a reminder of how much I'd lost. As a result, I grew angry, frustrated, and depressed. Paul was the one who had broken the faith, yet I was the one whose life had been turned upside down. Paul was still in his house. Paul still had his job. Paul still had his full income. On top of everything else, Paul still had all of *my* stuff, too. It wasn't fair, and I didn't hesitate to tell God how I felt.

It was during this month in my Bible reading plan that the schedule had me in the book of Job. I thought, *You've got to be kidding me. Here I am, in a major emotional funk, and now I have to read about Job and all of his suffering?* I nearly decided to skip Job and move on to the next book in the schedule, but something kept me there. I'd never read Job's story; honestly, I'd always avoided it. I'd heard teaching on it before, and I'd heard other people's testimonies about their own seasons in the valley and what a blessing it had been for them, but I always secretly hoped I wouldn't have to walk in those shoes. I foolishly thought that if I spent time studying Job and his story, that God would lead me into that kind of a season as an object lesson, so I avoided it at all costs.

As it turned out, Job was the perfect companion. Who better to be by your side during the lowest point in your life than someone who survived their own valley season? It reminds me of a story told during an episode of *The West Wing* television series: *A man was walking along the street when he fell into a deep pit. A doctor walked by and the man called out to him for help.*

The doctor wrote out a prescription, dropped it into the pit, and walked on. A priest then walked by and the man again called out for help. The priest wrote out a prayer, dropped it into the pit, and continued walking. Finally, one of the man's friends walks by. The man calls out, "Hey Joe, it's me, Fred. Can you help me out?" His friend immediately jumps down into the pit and joins him. "Are you crazy?" Fred exclaims. "What did you do that for? Now we're both here in the pit." "Yeah," Joe replies, "but I've been down here before, and I know the way out!"[11]

Job isn't held up as an example for the rest of us because he denied what had happened to him. He didn't thank God for allowing the enemy to wreck everything in his life. He didn't put on a happy face while he was in agony inside. Job is an example to us because he was *real with God* in the midst of horrific circumstances. All of his children were killed. His business and wealth were destroyed in an instant. His health went in the tank. We read that even his wife and friends were sources of tension and stress during this time. Job got angry. Job got frustrated. Job got depressed. Job even threw a pity party for himself, and that's when I really started to connect with him. In Job 29, he laments the good old days before tragedy struck:

*Oh that I were as in months gone by, as in the days
when God watched over me… as I was in the prime
of my days, when the friendship of God was over my
tent…* (Job 29:2, 4)

His words mirrored my heart during those months
in the apartment. I ached for the life I'd had in Folsom
before I met Paul, and reading Job's words gave me
the freedom to fully feel that hurt.

I used to try and make myself feel better when
feeling depressed or sorry for myself. I would tell
myself to snap out of it, and remind myself of all the
other people who were worse off than me. I never
gave myself permission to have a bad day. There was
grace for everyone else, but never any for me. In Job's
story, I saw that it was not only ok, but healthy, for me
to experience deep sorrow. It was ok for me to grieve
the loss of the life I'd had. While it was true that my
own folly had led me into marriage with Paul, and I
had some responsibility for my current circumstances,
it was also true that I'd been deceived and hurt by
Paul and had suffered real loss. It was ok to acknowl-
edge that and respond to it with sorrow and grief.

It was during this time that I also found myself
thinking about John quite a bit. It had been six years
since he had passed away, and I couldn't figure out

why he was on my mind so much in those days. But in going through the grieving process for all that I'd lost in Folsom, I was also being given an opportunity to fully mourn the loss of John. I hadn't really done that when he died in 2005. Once the memorial service was over, I had shifted right into recovery mode and never looked back. I donated his things and started packing away his memory. I never took an appropriate amount of time to process through the end of our marriage and the hole it had left in my life, but when things fell apart with Paul, my heart was broken wide open and out of that chasm old hurts and losses came up, including John's death.

October 2011 was a raw and emotional time for me. I felt like a train wreck most of the time—a walking mass of devastation. I didn't know it, but I was just steps from the lowest and darkest point in my entire journey.

I never used to understand how someone got to a point where they thought suicide was the best option to solve whatever problems they were facing—until I briefly considered it myself.

It was a Saturday night in late October or early November. I'd been sitting in my living room for who knows how long, just crying. I don't recall any one specific thought that started it all, but then again, there wasn't exactly a shortage of problems in my life at that time. I hated my apartment, and I wasn't wild about the work I was doing. I was splitting my time between the Folsom office and corporate headquarters in Orange County, and was getting pressured to move down there full time, which I absolutely did not want to do. I'd also started weekly counseling sessions, and we were in the process of exploring old wounds. On top of it all, my communication with Paul had turned even more contentious than usual.

After plans for a visit had fallen through, not once but twice, Paul was threatening to file for divorce and drag it out for as long as possible. He told me he had the money to do it and he didn't care how long it took. I was exhausted from fighting on so many different fronts, and his threat was the straw that broke the camel's back. Every conversation with Paul was difficult and every day was hard. The thought of facing a long, drawn out divorce was more than I could take.

But I wasn't just fighting Paul; I was fighting myself. My head and heart were duking it out in a battle royale, one telling me I needed to dump Paul as quickly as possible and the other clinging to the marriage for dear life. My head wanted to tell Paul to go to hell and just be done with him, but my heart still held out hope that we might reconcile and I might be able to return to Washington. I hated my current situation so much that going back to Paul and settling for life with him actually seemed palatable. *At least*, I thought, *I'd be back in a nicer home. At least I'd be back in the Pacific Northwest. At least I wouldn't have to work. At least I wouldn't be alone and I wouldn't be facing a legal battle.*

I could take the easy way out and reconcile with Paul, and settle for a "less than" existence, or I could keep fighting for what I knew was right and wise. I was just so tired; I couldn't see an end in sight. Every time I thought about my life, I just felt hopeless and trapped. That Saturday night, I just wanted to be done. As I sat in my chair, head in my hands, I thought about how great it would be to just stop fighting. I could just give up on everything, including life. I could rest and be at peace. With my eyes closed, I could imagine the silence. It was so attractive right then, I didn't even want to open my eyes. I didn't want the tiniest sliver of reality to interrupt my reverie.

In that moment of darkness, God showed up and a picture began to take shape. I was standing on a dirt path. To my left, the path and everything around it was engulfed in blackness. I couldn't see anything more than just a few feet beyond me. To my right, I couldn't see anything but the path itself, but it looked as though it made its way upward, and it was well lit. Somewhere in the back of my mind, I knew I was being given a choice: life or death. At that moment, it was an all or nothing choice, but every day we face life or death decisions. Deuteronomy 30:19-20 says:

> *…therefore choose life that you may live… that you may love the Lord your God, that you may obey His voice, and that you may hold fast to Him… for He is your life and the length of your days.*

We are constantly given opportunities to follow God into life, or follow the world, our flesh, and the enemy into death. Often, following God is the more difficult choice and that's why giving up is so tempting. It's hard to fight the good fight of faith. I'm sure that's why I started to cry again as I looked at the path before me. I knew in that moment I would choose life, and I knew things would continue to be hard for a while. Surrender is like that. Our flesh wants the easy way out, and when we crucify it in order to follow God, we grieve another little death of the self. We mourn the loss of comfort, safety, and security.

I opened my eyes then and saw my cell phone sitting on the arm of the chair. I picked it up and sent out a text message to five or six friends, all godly women who knew the details of my circumstances. I told them I was having a really bad night and that I was in pain, and I asked them all to pray for me. In a matter of minutes, I received several responses, all full of hope, encouragement and love. When the enemy is looking to take us out of the picture, the last thing he wants us doing is reaching out to other believers for help. He will try to shame us out of doing it, and try to make us believe that others won't accept us if they see our pain and suffering. He will try to isolate us and then pick us apart until he's destroyed us. I didn't really want anyone else to know how badly I was hurting that night. I was feeling raw and vulnerable, and a part of me was embarrassed to ask for help—but we don't grow in a vacuum, and God didn't design us to live as an island. He wired us for fellowship, for deep and intimate relationship with other people, and it's not just for our own benefit. The next morning at New Song, one of the friends I had texted pulled me aside and gave me a hug. She then said something I'll never forget. She told me that while she understood

I was in a whole lot of pain at that time, she was also encouraged to see that I didn't have it all together. She said I had always looked like I had this perfect little life with God, and she was relieved to see that I experienced struggles and dark moments. My willingness to be vulnerable and transparent had given her hope as she faced her own tough seasons in life.

That Sunday afternoon, as I stood in my apartment watching the sunset, God spoke to me once again. It was as clear as that day in June when He told me I had to leave Paul. Leaning against the door frame of the slider, I clearly sensed God on my right as He put His arm around my shoulders and whispered, "Breakthroughs will come. Breakthroughs *will* come." For the first time in months, I felt hopeful. God had promised, and Hebrews 10:23 tells us that "He who promised is faithful." I didn't know how and I didn't know when, but I knew in that moment that God was going to take care of everything. I was still exhausted and I still felt as though I'd been through the wringer, but I knew God would get me through it somehow.

It would take weeks for me to fully comprehend the fact that I had contemplated suicide, even if only for the briefest moment. To this day, I'm grateful for the lesson that night. Suicide isn't an option that people choose after logical and deliberate consideration; it is an escape from pain. For some, it's physical pain and for others, it's emotional pain. Anyone who has chosen that route has been suffering and they simply wish to be free of their circumstances. I didn't give any thought to those who would be left behind. All I could see was my pain, and my only thought was to be at rest. I suppose that's why suicide is often seen as a selfish act, but it's really one of desperation. In the same way that people jump from the window of a burning building, a hurting person is looking to escape an equally desperate and fearful circumstance—and we cannot possibly know or understand that kind of pain point until we ourselves are standing on that ledge.

Chapter 18
"COME, LET US REASON TOGETHER"

For several months after my return to Folsom, Paul and I continued to communicate. While I quickly realized that even physical distance had done nothing to improve his behavior, I held out hope that things would change. I was still willing to ride the roller-coaster of Paul's presence in my life.

Early on, I made the decision to end the marriage, but it was really more of a reaction than a decision; that's why, ultimately, it didn't stick. I could see that Paul's behavior wasn't changing and it was hard to miss God putting verse after verse in front of me about false prophets and divisive people. Still, I hung on to the dream of living happily ever after with Paul in Washington. Every day was a battle. Physically leaving Paul was just the first of many skirmishes.

There would later be fights to leave him emotionally, legally, and spiritually, in that order.

Satan had dangled just the right bait to get me to leave Folsom in the first place and take me out of God's will. Now that I was back in Folsom, and really making an effort to seek God and follow Him, the enemy wasn't going to let that happen without a fight. In the months after I returned, the enemy used Paul to come at me from several different angles. Paul sent me flowers and love letters. He emailed me his notes from devotionals he was reading. He started attending a new church in Washington and mailed me CDs of their sermons. He began talking to me about what had happened between us in deeply spiritual terms. On the surface, it appeared he was changing, but in between all these things his old behaviors would continue to crop up. He would speak to me in accusatory tones and tell me that I wasn't hearing from God correctly. He would make excuses for his behavior, blaming it on ADHD and demon possession. In one breath, he would tell me that he believed my leaving him had been God's will; in the next, he would contradict himself and tell me that he had forgiven me for leaving him, implying that it hadn't been God's will.

It's easy to look at my journal entries from that time and see the pattern of behavior now, but in the midst of it I was terribly confused. I wondered at times if Paul was right and I was hearing from God all wrong, and I questioned my motives for staying in California. When Paul was being nice to me, I thought maybe God was finally changing his heart, but after relapsing into old behaviors, we would travel the same old path once again. It was just like the relationship between King Saul and David. Saul was constantly chasing after David trying to kill him. When David would call him on it, Saul would immediately confess that he was in the wrong, telling David that he (David) was more righteous and apologizing all over himself.[12] Soon after, though, Saul went right back to hunting down David and making another attempt to kill him. Over and over, they repeated this pattern of Saul operating out of his emotions and David responding in wisdom and discernment. Saul's behavior never changed because he was never genuinely repentant. He was never willing to turn away from his behavior and allow God to change his heart. He never dealt with the source of his behavior; consequently, he continued to repeat it.

I'd like to tell you that I responded to Paul with as much wisdom as David, but the truth is that I had no boundaries and I usually let Paul back into my heart and my life with each little change in his behavior.

I always invited him all the way back in without gauging whether or not it was safe or appropriate to do so. That, in turn, gave false hope and encouragement to Paul. On one particular visit that summer, we drove to a mountain lake for the afternoon. We took a walk around the lake and spent some time reading the Bible. Our discussions all centered on spiritual matters and I thought that maybe Paul was beginning to experience some real change in his life. He returned to Washington believing that we were on the road to reconciliation. After he left, though, I realized that the practical side of things hadn't been addressed. Paul wanted to hide out in his spiritual bubble and use his relationship *with* God to hide *from* God. He didn't want to pursue counseling and do the hard work of looking at his brokenness, and I knew that would be necessary in order to consider reconciliation. I told Paul as much in one of our phone calls the following week; it was no surprise that Paul was angry and frustrated by my retreat from him once again. There simply was no consistency in either one of us during this time. We were both wishy-washy and double-minded.

Our unhealthy dance would continue into the holidays and culminate in a Thanksgiving visit which would finally lead me out of reactions and into decisions.

November 6, 2011 marked one year of being married to Paul. I never imagined that we would spend it separated and in such turmoil. We had been out of touch for a few weeks, and I knew better than to reach out to him that night. It seemed like every time I made an effort to communicate with Paul, God put a verse in front of me about false prophets, lying, and deceit. The spiritual tug o' war happening inside of me was unlike anything I'd ever experienced. The battle lines were so clear. You'd think I would have easily realized that Paul wasn't a healthy person. I actually did know that, but letting go of him was very difficult for me. I wasn't emotionally healthy myself, and I was still fighting my own old habits and hang-ups. It was that part of me that won out and sent Paul an email acknowledging our anniversary and asking how he'd been. Part of my reason for writing to him stemmed from my lack of boundaries. I knew that he would be hurt if I didn't send some kind of note to him on that date. I knew that I would probably hear from him a day or two later with some kind of rebuke about being so cold that I couldn't even wish him a happy anniversary, so I violated what I knew I shouldn't do in order to avoid Paul's inevitable reply, which I wasn't responsible for in the first place.

But poor boundaries were only part of the reason I wrote to him. As crazy as it sounds, I still loved Paul and I was still hoping for reconciliation. I hated that we were at such odds with one another. I knew Paul wasn't a wicked or evil person; he was just foolish and immature. There had been some good things in Paul's behavior and I didn't want to give up until I knew I had exhausted every avenue. I wanted Paul to get into counseling and get the help he needed, but I couldn't want it for him, and I certainly couldn't do it for him.

After I sent the email, I sat down to work on that day's Bible reading and journaling. Sure enough, God put a few verses in front of me that clearly spoke into what I had just done:

Are you so foolish… did you suffer so many things in vain…? (Gal 3:3, 4)

Deliver my soul, O Lord, from lying lips, from a deceitful tongue… too long has my soul had its dwelling with those who hate peace. I am for peace, but when I speak, they are for war. (Psalms 120:2, 6, 7)

I sighed. I felt like a wave—rolling in to shore and then back out—reaching out to Paul and then retreating. Why couldn't I just stay away from him?

Paul wrote back that week, and we began communicating again. Things were a bit more civil this time around and I felt comfortable enough to invite him down for a visit at Thanksgiving. As I mentioned before, I didn't know how to let Paul in just a little bit; it was always an all-or-nothing deal. For this visit, I didn't ask him to stay in a hotel. I let him stay with me in my apartment, and we made plans to drive down to San Francisco for a couple of days and stay in a hotel near the coast. We had dinner with my family on Thanksgiving then drove to the Bay Area on Friday. It was a really nice visit, but that's only because we chose to ignore the elephant in the room and didn't come close to discussing our situation. I came to realize later that Paul and I would have been great together if all we'd chosen to do was go out on dates. Paul was really good at having fun; what he wasn't so hot at was being in a committed relationship with someone and investing himself in that. Since all we did was sightsee, go out to eat, and talk about everything except us, San Francisco was a good trip. However, all that changed on Sunday.

Things were good until we left to go shopping before we took in a movie. On the drive to the store, we got to talking about what was next for us. Paul wasn't comfortable with ambiguity. He was always pressuring me for definite answers. When was I going to be done processing through my hurt? When did I think I'd be ready to come back? He always wanted specifics and I often couldn't give them. I had no idea how long it was going to take me to work through the betrayal, and it frustrated Paul to no end when I would tell him, "I don't know." He saw it as avoidance, but it was just the truth of how I felt at that time. I don't remember the specifics of our discussion, but part of it involved me offering up several possible outcomes for our relationship, including me remaining in California long-term while we worked through counseling. Paul immediately latched onto that outcome, which he saw as the least favorable for him. Like a dog with a bone, he refused to let go. He wanted to know why I had included it, what was I thinking about it, and was that the direction I wanted to go? I tried to get him to see that it was just one of a few outcomes and that nothing was guaranteed. But that wasn't good enough, and for the remainder of that day and night, we spiraled down into the ugliest disagreement we'd had to date. Because Paul hadn't gotten a hotel, I couldn't get away. I kept trying to end the discussion, but Paul was relentless. Finally, somewhere around midnight, I told Paul we had to get some sleep.

When we got up the next morning, things were still tense and I noticed that Paul wasn't packing his bag. I had agreed to drive him to the airport on my way to work, and kept prompting him to pack. For some reason, this made him even more upset. When he wanted to leave some of his things with me in the apartment, I refused and asked him to pack up everything he'd brought with him and take it back. I didn't know if or when he would be visiting again, and I didn't want to hold on to his stuff. We drove to the airport in near silence and I dropped him off. As I drove to work, I think a bit of delayed shock began to set in. I started trembling and crying, wondering how things had gone downhill so suddenly. I had been so frustrated during the argument. Everything I said had been misunderstood, misconstrued, and misinterpreted. No matter how thoroughly I tried to explain myself, it did absolutely no good. Despite my efforts to understand Paul's perspective, it wasn't good enough for him. There simply had been no way for me to win.

I got to work and stumbled around through my day. Paul and I had been in countless arguments, but this one was different; I wasn't bouncing back from it like I had the others. This one had struck a deep nerve and it wasn't letting go. When I got home, I opened the front door and just stood there for a minute. From the entry, you could see nearly the entire apartment: the living room, dining room, and a good portion of the bedroom. As I stood there, I took in the sight of the mess my place had been left in after Paul's visit. God burned that image into my brain. I realized it was a perfect picture of what my life was like every time I let Paul back into it — he came in, made a mess, and then I was left to clean up the damage, both physical and emotional.

Something shifted inside me that weekend; it was subtle, but it was there. The scales had finally tipped in favor of leaving Paul for good, but it would still be another few weeks before I'd be at peace with that decision.

The visit at Thanksgiving really got me thinking about why I hadn't yet decided to leave Paul. I started to question why I continued to put myself in harm's way. Why did I want to stay with him?

Paul was scheduled to come back for one more visit the following weekend. In the aftermath of our holiday meltdown, I was dreading the visit. I had emailed Paul right after the Thanksgiving visit and laid down some ground rules. I wasn't going to tolerate the kind of chaos that had ensued the previous Sunday. First, I needed him to stay in a hotel, and second, I wasn't willing to be his emotional punching bag any longer. If he was going to toss around accusations and such, I wasn't going to engage with him. I had also asked him to confirm whether or not he was actually going to make the trip in light of how things had ended on Sunday. I never did hear from him and began to wonder if he might not make the trip. Unfortunately, that's just how Paul was. I assumed he had canceled, but early on Saturday morning my phone began to ring. It was Paul, and he was at the airport wondering where I was.

When I explained that he hadn't confirmed his plans, he began to lay into me. I took a deep breath, reminded him that I wasn't going to let him speak to me that way, and ended the call. It was the first time in my life I can recall enforcing a boundary so clearly. I stood there in my apartment, shaking from the effort. I knew Paul would be calling back, but instead of waiting for it, I went back to getting ready for the day. I would go and pick him up, but it would be on my terms. When I listened to his voice mail messages — there had been several — he was pleading with me to not leave him stranded at the airport. I called him back, told him I hadn't planned on abandoning him, and reminded him yet again that I wasn't going to tolerate his accusations. After picking him up at the airport, we stopped for breakfast on the way back to town. I asked him where he was staying and he just gave me this irritated look. I said, "You didn't book a hotel room, did you?" "No," came the terse reply. I held firm to my decision and told Paul I'd help him find a place to stay, but it wasn't going to be in my apartment again.

He launched into another round of manipulation, saying that he may as well just go back to the airport and fly home if that's how things were going to be. "Fine," I replied, "your choice. I can take you back to the airport or I can take you to a hotel. It's up to you." He opted for the hotel and we later attended a prayer and healing event at a nearby church. I had hoped we would get prayer and maybe some counseling while there, and we did, but it was more of the same old routine. In the brief time we had with the counselor, you could see even they were growing frustrated with Paul's unwillingness to own his issues. He flew home the next day, and I was left to wrestle through the questions I had about staying in the marriage.

Over the next couple of weeks, I spent my drives to and from work talking it out with God. Each day, I'd bring my reasons for staying with Paul and each day we would wrestle them out. In Isaiah 1:18, the Lord says, "Come, let us reason together." God created us with an intellect and a brain, and it wasn't to just take up space in our skull. He also doesn't expect blind obedience. He gave us free will, and it's most pleasing to Him when we exercise it and *choose* to trust and obey. I believe God was pleased that I took the time to meet with Him during those weeks in order to come to a thoughtful and prayerful decision regarding my marriage.

Because of those conversations with God, I was able to see that the root of each reason was fear. I was afraid to be alone. I was afraid of struggling financially. I was afraid of the legal battle that loomed ahead. I was afraid of facing an unknown future. I wanted to stay with Paul because I feared the alternatives, not because there was anything particularly appealing about life with him under the current circumstances. God talks about fear quite a lot in the

Bible. Usually, He is telling His people to "fear not" and "be courageous." About two weeks into my conversations with God, He put two verses in front of me, one before I made my decision and one after. The first was Hebrews 10:38-39 which reads, "But my righteous one shall live by faith… we are not of those who shrink back to destruction."

The same night I read those verses from Hebrews, I had also been praying for a friend's sister. She had recently landed in jail, and the Holy Spirit led me to start praying through the story of the prodigal son on her behalf. As I prayed about how there was nothing that she'd done that God wouldn't forgive, and that He was waiting to embrace her if she would just turn to Him, my own words rang in my ears and I knew without a doubt God meant that prayer for me. I had the sudden and clear realization that God wasn't mad at me for how I'd spent the previous 18 months. He still loved me, and He had been waiting for me to make the decision to leave Paul and return to Him. It wasn't until that night that God showed me I had been trying so hard to stay with Paul because I felt it was the penance I had to pay. I had been trying to punish myself for my own folly. *I had made my bed, and now I had to lie in it.* But God showed me grace that night. He made it clear that I had been forgiven, and that Jesus' work on the cross had been enough. There was no more condemnation. There was no penance required. However, God didn't stop there. I sensed that He was also giving me permission to walk into a healthier future. It was ok for me to desire a better life, and to desire wholeness and wellness for myself. God desires that we would be holy as He is holy.[13] Holiness is wholeness; it is being complete in Christ, and I didn't have to feel guilty about desiring that any longer.

Leaving the marriage was the only decision rooted in love. Staying in an unhealthy and invalid marriage is not something that a loving God would have me do. It wasn't something that I would do out of love for myself, either — and it was the most loving thing I could do for Paul. Sometimes, loving someone means getting out of the way so that God will have a clear shot with them.

I remember sitting at my writing desk, journal open, and just crying for a while as God lifted the guilt and shame I'd been carrying for so many months. Isaiah 61:1 tells us that Jesus came to proclaim freedom for captives and liberty for prisoners. One definition of that freedom is the ability to see clearly. God had most certainly given me a better perspective on my circumstances that night, and the ability to confidently and courageously make the decision to end my marriage. The very next night, my Bible reading plan had me in Hebrews 13, and verse 6 was timely encouragement for what lay ahead: "The Lord is my helper... I will not be afraid. What will man do to me?"

It had been six months, almost to the day, since I'd left Washington. In that time, I'd waffled back and forth between ending the marriage and pursuing reconciliation. I'd been utterly torn between the two choices, never being able to commit to one or the other. Every time I chose one, I immediately began to question my decision. I'd been operating out of my emotions, reacting to my circumstances and Paul's ever-changing behavior. It wasn't until I earnestly sought out Jesus and engaged with Him — directly in conversation and through His Word — that I was able to make a decision anchored in Him and in His truth. It was only then that I experienced peace in the decision, and it was only then that I was able to move ahead with a clear conscience about that decision.

Healing is a process, sometimes a long and painful one; it's not like flipping a switch and then we're healed. It took me six months to finally decide I'd had enough. Not coincidentally, I hadn't been eligible to file for an annulment during that time because I hadn't yet met the residency requirements in California.

But trust me, I had tried. During those six months, I met with an attorney and I met with one of those do-it-yourself agencies that reviews your paperwork and offers advice. More than likely, had I been successful I would have regretted the hasty decision and might have questioned the outcome for who knows how long. God, in His grace, protected me from that. In needing to wait six months to meet the residency requirements, God gave me the time to fully process and evaluate things so that I would have no doubts or regrets—and I didn't. That night in my bedroom, the decision had become crystal clear.

Chapter 19

CALLING IT QUITS

Ask, and it will be given to you; seek, and you will find; knock, and it will be opened to you. For everyone who asks receives, and he who seeks finds, and to him who knocks it will be opened. **– Matthew 7:7-8**

As I researched options for filing the annulment, I found a small piece of California family law which confirmed the invalidity of my marriage to Paul. I'd known it from a common sense standpoint all along, but finding the legal foundation for the annulment helped strengthen my resolve to end the marriage. My research also led me to the conclusion that I would need a lawyer. Paul was still refusing me access to the house so I could get my things, and quite frankly, I wanted to have as little contact with him as possible during this process. Two weeks after praying and asking God to provide the right attorney who would also be affordable, a friend from church offered me the name of her lawyer. John turned out to be great. He was very down to earth and had a no-nonsense approach to things. He laid out a simple but effective plan for filing the paperwork and getting my things back. When it came time to talk about his fees, the total estimated cost was still more than I had in savings, but far less than the previous quote I'd received the year before from another attorney. I made the off-hand remark that if I could charge it, I'd go ahead and give him the retainer that day. As it turned out, he *did* take credit cards. I wasn't wild about adding to my debt, but I believed he was the right person for the job and I wanted to get started with things. By early February, we were ready to serve the petition on Paul. In it, we had included a motion for a hearing to get my things, and that motion included a monetary penalty if Paul refused me further access to the house. God, though, had other plans.

On February 11, I got a phone call from Paul's son-in-law telling me Paul was in the hospital with a bad case of pneumonia; so bad, in fact, he was on a respirator. He and Paul's daughter were calling to get the gate code for the community where we'd lived so they could collect some of his things. After our conversation, I wondered how Paul's daughter was doing. I knew from my own experience with my second husband that hospital stays were nerve-wracking and there was always more to manage than you realized. I called her back about an hour later and asked if she wanted me to fly up and help her. I could hear the relief in her voice as she accepted my offer, and an hour later I was booked on the first flight out the next morning.

I'd only met "Nancy" on two previous occasions when I was living in Washington. Things had been a little awkward during those meetings, so I wasn't quite sure what to expect when I got to the hospital. Fortunately, Paul's circumstances served as a bridge where we could meet and get reacquainted. That proved especially helpful once Paul's other daughter arrived from Texas. I'd never met "Lisa" and only knew her by reputation. I was extremely anxious about meeting her, but God worked everything out. Despite all of the potential for things to have gone sideways, especially since Paul and I were separated at the time, all of us ended up getting along quite nicely. Nancy and her husband even invited me to stay at Paul's house that week—and that was how, after eight months of being powerless to retrieve my things, God Himself opened the door and made it possible. Not only that, but God inspired my sister and brother-in-law to drive up with their SUV later that week and help me bring back the most essential items.

There are some things that I find important and interesting to note about this particular trip. First, I didn't go up to Washington with the express intent to retrieve my things; I went up there to help Nancy and be of service. Second, I went despite my fears and anxieties. Not only did I not know how Nancy and Lisa would receive me, but anyone who knows me will tell you how much I fear airline travel. I also didn't know what to expect with Paul. I knew he was going to be on a respirator, but I didn't know how much we would be able to communicate. He ended up being pretty well sedated the entire week I was there and the respirator allowed for no verbal communication. On a few occasions, he was alert enough to communicate with hand signals, but that was about it. I left Seattle on Thursday afternoon with my sister and brother-in-law, and I heard from Nancy on Friday that Paul had finally been taken off the respirator and was able to talk. Looking back, it seems that Paul being on a respirator was God's way of protecting me during the week I was there. Had he been able to talk, he probably would have stopped Nancy from letting me stay in the house and might have poisoned the time I had with Nancy, her husband and Lisa. Because I was able to interact with them directly, God used that week to build a connection between us that hadn't been possible when I'd been living with Paul. That connection led to several follow up phone calls with Nancy where both of us learned the truth about circumstances surrounding my marriage to Paul. Those truths, in turn, helped both of us heal and move forward.

Much of my time that week was spent with Paul in his hospital room while his kids cleaned up the house and got it ready for his return. I wrote earlier about my own introduction to Paul's housekeeping skills, but things had just gone downhill after I left. I had offered to help while I was there, but the girls insisted it was their responsibility and told me that it would be most helpful if I could simply sit with Paul, keep him company, and let them know how he was doing. During that week, God gave me the opportunity to love Paul in a way I didn't think was possible. Despite the lies, the deception, and the countless hurtful comments, God gave me the grace to serve him that week. I sat by his bed and held his hand, I wiped down his face and arms when he ran a fever, I calmed him down when he grew anxious about the breathing tube, and I sent away technicians when Paul was too agitated for procedures. In Matthew 5:44, Jesus tells His listeners to love their enemies and pray for those who persecute them. I'd been angry with Paul for so long, and up until just a few weeks before this trip, I'd still been lamenting the unfairness of the entire situation. But in my willingness to set aside my own agenda, God was able to use me to serve Paul and his family. That's when Paul's daughters were able to see Jesus and that's when God was glorified.

By the end of the week, both of his daughters had commented on how unusual they found it that I would come up and serve Paul like that under the circumstances. They didn't know all the details, but they knew enough to know that not everyone would have changed their plans on a dime to come up and take care of someone who had treated them so badly for so long. Both girls also commented that they wanted to stay in touch, and they made sure we all exchanged current contact information. The entire week was full of outcomes I could never have predicted — getting on an airplane, staying at the house, getting my things back, loving and serving someone who had hurt me, and getting into relationship with Paul's daughters — but that week was just one example of why we know Ephesians 3:20 is true. God really is the One who is able to do exceedingly and abundantly more than we can think or ask.

After Paul's hospital stay, his demeanor towards me became much friendlier. I'd like to say that the change was permanent, but it wasn't. As soon as he realized that I still wasn't willing to reconcile with him, things went back to the way they'd been.

For the next couple of months, the attorney tried to get Paul served. After several unsuccessful attempts, I began to worry that it would never happen. In early May, John suggested he contact Paul and ask if he would be willing to voluntarily receive service through certified mail. Surprisingly, he agreed, but the next day he called me and wanted to know what was in the petition. I suggested that he call the attorney and have him explain it, but he refused. When I tried to outline the details of the petition, the call turned nasty and Paul began to once again blast me with accusations and hurtful remarks. As the week progressed, John and I waited for the signature receipt on the certified packet but it never came. Without that receipt, we had no way to prove Paul had gotten the documents, and we couldn't move ahead with the annulment.

I was beyond frustrated. I was upset that we were having trouble getting Paul served, but more than that, I realized how angry I was about the whole situation. The more I thought about it, the more it dawned on me that I'd never been able to be the victim. I was always so busy with Paul playing the victim that I'd never gotten to deal with my own hurt in the betrayal, and I was mad. On May 14, I journaled, *Lord, how do I deal with all this? How do I release all this anger, frustration, and unforgiveness towards Paul?* Over the next day, God reminded me of Judas' betrayal, Peter's denial, and the disciples' abandonment. He brought to mind all the times that Jesus dealt with the Pharisees, and all the difficult conversations that had taken place between them. He had been there, I realized, and He knew what I was going through. On May 15, I wrote, *Maybe this is the first part of healing – realizing that You have been there, that You have already experienced my pain, my hurt, my anger and my frustration. In spite of all that, You forgave fully. And since You did, there is power for me to do it, too… Jesus went through all that He did so that He would understand when we came to Him in our own pain. He allows us to go through painful situations so that we might grow in understanding, as well, and be a comfort and support to others in their time of need.*

The next day, I heard a sermon on the radio about suffering, and how God sometimes doesn't take it away; rather, He uses it to transform us and glorify

Himself. As I listened to the message, I began to realize that suffering draws us close to Christ and it brings us into communion with Him. The apostle Paul wrote about this dynamic in 2 Corinthians 1:5-6:

> *For just as the sufferings of Christ are ours in abundance, so also our comfort is abundant through Christ. But if we are afflicted, it is for your comfort and salvation; or if we are comforted, it is for your comfort, which is effective in the patient enduring of the same sufferings which we also suffer...*

Peter, too, wrote about sharing in Christ's suffering. In 1 Peter 4:12-13, he wrote:

> *Beloved, do not be surprised at the fiery ordeal among you, which comes upon you for your testing, as though some strange thing were happening to you; but to the degree that you share the sufferings of Christ, keep on rejoicing, so that also at the revelation of His glory you may rejoice with exultation.*

We're all pretty quick to jump on board the glory bandwagon, but less so when it comes to sharing in Christ's suffering. However, it's in the trenches of war, in the midst of trial and suffering, where you really begin to draw near to Jesus. That's when you start to realize that God isn't punishing you. It's not God on one side of the fence and you on the other side, suffering at His hand; rather, He is there suffering *with* you and fighting alongside you. It's the two of you in it together, and His presence is your strength and encouragement.

On May 19, God gave us the break we needed. Out of the blue, I got a call from the hospital in Washington. It was an emergency room nurse calling to confirm one of Paul's medications. I was more than a little confused, but then she went on to say that Paul and I had skipped some information on the intake form when he'd been admitted to the hospital earlier that day. Apparently, someone had taken Paul to the hospital and this nurse assumed I was that woman. My contact information must still have been in the system from when I'd visited back in February and that's how the nurse had gotten my phone number. After the call, I realized God had just provided a way for me to get Paul served. He would be captive in his hospital room for at least a few days, it seemed, since he was back in for pneumonia. I immediately got on the phone to my attorney, gave him the address for the hospital and told him to get Paul served just as quickly as he could. I'll admit that part of me felt like a real jerk for having him served in a hospital, of all places. But, I'd already suspended activity on the petition once when Paul had been hospitalized in February and I hadn't been rewarded for that effort. It was time to get things done, and if God was opening a door for me, I was going to step through.

Three days later, Paul was served in the hospital. As you might imagine, I got quite the earful. I was blamed for causing the heart attack he claimed he'd had during that hospital stay, and I was blamed for the increased costs of the petition. He threatened to file a response and drag out the process for as long as he could. Over the next couple of weeks, though, we eventually came to a truce. I agreed to cover all legal costs and return my wedding ring. In exchange, Paul agreed to not file a response and let the judgment go to default. Realizing that I wasn't going to change my mind about the marriage, Paul asked if we might try being friends. I was tired of being at odds with him, so I agreed to give it a try. I thought that without the pressure of reconciliation hanging over our heads, we might be able to relax and actually grow a friendship. The problem is that friendship, like marriage, requires trust and the ability to invest yourself in the relationship. Friendship also requires boundaries. Up until now, Paul hadn't demonstrated any of these qualities. It was foolish of me to think things would really be different as friends, but part of me was just buying time until the 30-day response period for the petition was over. I didn't want to do anything to rock the boat with Paul until I knew it was too late for him to file a response.

It's hard to be friends with a former spouse, especially when the issues that led you to end the marriage haven't been addressed. It had been two weeks since I agreed to try friendship with Paul, and it really wasn't working for me. I figured we would communicate occasionally, but Paul wanted to exchange text messages all day long, every day. At first, I responded to his texts pretty quickly, but when I realized he was taking a mile after being offered an inch, I started to back off and reply less frequently.

One day while running errands, I heard a Christian legal program on the radio. At the moment I tuned in, the caller was a man going through a separation from his wife. Everything he said mirrored my side of the conversations I'd had with Paul and with my friends. His wife, ironically, had been behaving much like Paul. As this guy finished up his story, the lawyer advised him to break things off with his wife. Her behavior clearly indicated she wasn't interested in changing anything. She just wanted to keep doing what she'd been doing, no matter how hurtful it was to this guy. It was an incredibly toxic relationship and this poor guy just kept giving her chance after chance while accepting her verbal abuse and disrespectful attitude. I remember that I turned off the radio when I first started listening to his story. It was so much like my own story. I thought, *I've been living this. I don't need to listen to someone else's grief.* But just as quickly, I knew it wasn't a coincidence. I knew I needed to hear his story and tune in to whatever God wanted to tell me. As the lawyer gave her advice, I knew God was telling me I needed to completely close off communication with Paul. It had been a year since I'd left Washington and not one thing had changed. I'd known this for a while, but had been avoiding the decision. Part of the reason was that I was still a week out from the end of the 30-day response time for the petition, and I didn't want Paul so upset that he would file the response document.

That night, Paul and I were scheduled to talk on the phone. I very politely explained to him that communicating every day was a little much for me, and that I needed some space. That, of course, didn't go over well with Paul. He spent the next two hours reading me the riot act before reluctantly agreeing to less communication. We ended the call, and as I sat on the edge of my bed, I realized that I didn't feel much relief. I still felt like I had the sword of Damocles hanging over my head.

The next morning, before church, I was going through my scheduled Bible reading which had me in 1 Kings 20. The chapter starts out with a story between the King of Aram and the King of Israel. The Aramean king sends word to Israel that he wants their silver and gold, along with their wives and children. Israel agrees, but then the King of Aram sends word that his armies are going to invade and take not just the silver and gold, and wives and children, but everything they desire. In other words, he'd been given an inch but was now going to take a mile. The story immediately reminded me of Paul, and I wondered what else God was going to tell me. Near the end of the chapter, after God has given the Arameans into the hands of the Israelites, the King of Israel hears that the King of Aram is still alive. He sends for him, but instead of killing him he makes a covenant with him. One of the Jewish prophets then tells the king, "Thus says the Lord, 'Because you have let go out of your hand the man whom I had devoted to destruction, therefore your life shall go for his life, and your people for his people.'" I had no doubt that God was telling me I had compromised the night before in just asking for less communication with Paul. God had been leading me to sever *all* ties with Paul, and I had been disobedient.

I went on to church that morning, and I guess God knew I needed one more nudge. The pastor was talking about leadership, and how good leaders practice the axiom, "The buck stops here." Good leaders know when to make the tough calls. Right then, the pastor looked up into the congregation. Now, he may very well have been looking at someone other than me, but I would have sworn he was making direct eye contact with me when he said, "Sometimes, you have to make the call." Just moments before, I had tuned out from the sermon to contemplate how I was going to tell Paul that I couldn't have any more contact with him, and had begun thinking that I could just email or text him that decision. I remember sitting there, hearing those words, and actually holding my breath for a minute. It was one of those "God is totally talking to me right now" moments. I felt God's eyes on me, and I knew I needed to tell Paul over the phone. Mind you, I didn't want to; I'd never dreaded a call so much, but I had to own my decision and I needed to be an adult about it.

After church, I drove to a nearby park. I got Paul on the phone and broke the news. I told him I felt like it was God's leading to do this, and that I had been disobedient the night before. Ever since I'd left Washington, Paul had been telling me that I wasn't hearing from God correctly, and this decision just cemented that opinion in his mind. He let loose with a few more accusations and I finally just told him that I was sorry, but my mind was made up. I ended the call and prayed that God would stay Paul's hand from responding to the petition. God not only did that, but He also worked it out so that a hearing wasn't needed for the annulment. My attorney had told me that a hearing was customary for annulments, but I guess the paper trail was so clear in my case that the judge rendered his decision without it. After waiting just over a month for a hearing date, I received a surprise text from my lawyer on August 2, 2012, telling me that the annulment had been finalized and recorded the day before.

I stood there in my bedroom reading his message over and over. I'd been gearing up emotionally for the hearing and figured I still had more time to prepare for the official end of the marriage. I started to cry, then, as I realized that the fight was over. No more negotiations with Paul. No more calls. No more texts. I was finally free, and I was safe.

Chapter 20

A TIME TO GET WELL

It is difficult in the aftermath of choosing better. I thought I would be doing a happy dance. Instead, I am melancholy and I question if I did the right thing. A wise choice seems stubborn, and health feels like sickness. – **Journal entry, June 19, 2012**

2012 brought with it many changes in my life, none of which could have happened without the help of wise people God put in my path. Ellen was one such person. She was my Christian counselor for 15 months while I went through the biggest transitions in my journey. Up until that time in my life, I'd never been to a counselor or therapist. I always thought counseling was for other people with serious problems. I never saw my own life as being so messed up that I needed to meet with a counselor, but after returning from Washington, and being stripped of nearly everything in life, I knew it was time. I'd suffered the loss of three marriages and I was the common denominator. If I wanted my life to be different, I had to work on myself and my issues.

Many different kinds of therapy exist in the world. There's talk therapy. There's hypnotherapy. And there's no shortage of self-help therapy. Because of my Christian worldview, I knew that I wanted and needed God at the center of my counseling. He was my Creator and He knew me best. If I wanted to truly get to know myself, I needed to look to Him first and let Him lead me into a healthier way of thinking, responding, and behaving.

I had no idea what to expect. Quite frankly, I was a little terrified at the first appointment. When Ellen asked me what I hoped to accomplish in counseling, I honestly didn't know. I couldn't really come up with a good outcome for my time in therapy. After listening to me talk about where I was in life, and this was just three months after I'd returned to Folsom, in September 2011, she suggested that we explore the critical opinion I held towards myself and others. One of the first homework assignments she gave me was designed to help me be gracious with myself. I'd been talking about how disappointed I felt—and how I thought God must have felt—when I didn't adhere to a disciplined schedule of quiet time and journaling each day. I berated myself if I left it until just before bedtime because I saw it as squeezing in God before I called it a night, instead of making Him my priority first thing in the morning. Ellen told me that for the next week, I was to *stop* reading and journaling on a schedule. If I felt like doing it, great; if not, then I wasn't to force the issue and make myself do it out of obligation. I have to tell you, it felt pretty weird at first. I felt guilty for not doing it, *and* I felt guilty for the freedom I experienced. It was all new territory for me. I didn't know how to simply be with God. I'd always felt like I had to be doing something for Him. To not spend time reading or journaling, and still believe that He loved me and wasn't upset or disappointed with me was a huge breakthrough. That dynamic in my relationship with God wasn't completely fixed that week, but as Ellen liked to say, we planted a healthy stake and it would be something I could look back on as a mile marker in my journey into better emotional health.

One of the best things about therapy is that it provides a safe place for you to practice being vulnerable and authentic. I'd never really done that with God, and counseling gave me opportunities to let down my guard for an hour and cry or rant to my heart's content. I was safe with Ellen, covered in prayer and led by the Holy Spirit. There was no judgment, no condemnation, and no shame. There was just the space to be who I needed to be in those moments, and with every session I grew stronger in the truth that it was safe to be that way with God outside of my counseling appointments. Where I had believed that God was disappointed in me, I learned that He delighted in every aspect of me. Where I had believed that He was angry and waiting to punish me, I learned that He loved me at all times and was always ready to bless me with grace, mercy, and kindness. Coming into counseling, I had a very poor idea of who I was in Christ, but God was about to change all that with a prayer and visualization exercise that would radically change how I saw myself.

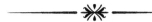

One of the exercises Ellen suggested for me was a rebirthing visualization. Because I had been conceived out of wedlock, and had always been told I was an accidental pregnancy, I felt like I didn't quite belong here in the world. My unplanned presence had driven me to pursue love, acceptance, and meaning in life, usually to my detriment. I needed a new picture of how I had come to be me. I needed to see myself from God's perspective.

When Ellen first told me about the exercise, I was leery. During the months I spent at the hypnotherapy school, I had gone through a similar exercise using hypnosis and past life regression, and Ellen's suggestion sounded a lot like my prior experience. After I shared my concerns with her, she explained the process in more detail and assured me it would be surrounded in prayer and would be Spirit-led. There was no hypnosis involved and no regression to an earlier time in life. The rebirthing exercise would be more like the quiet time I spent seeking God's voice.

I could see that Ellen believed in its benefits; part of me believed it, as well. After working through my fears and concerns regarding the process, we made plans to meet the next day and go through the exercise. When I arrived back at the church where Ellen had her office, I'm not sure if I was more scared or excited. I had a sense that something significant was about to happen, and I was looking forward to some breakthroughs in this area of life, but I was also afraid of what living from that new perspective would be like. You would think that embracing new and healthier attitudes would be easy for us, but it's not. Letting go of old, familiar ways is scary and awkward. There's always an adjustment period as we try out our new identity, and a measure of fear as we tread into unfamiliar territory.

As we began the exercise, Ellen explained the entire process. She would open with prayer and then read through a script describing each stage of my creation: conception, development, and birth. She would then check in with me at each stage to find out what I was seeing, hearing, and feeling to make sure we were constantly aligned with God and His truth, and to address things if we weren't. Ellen instructed me to close my eyes as she started describing God's work at my conception. Immediately, I saw Jesus with His arms outstretched, holding a treasure chest. A few years earlier, I had been doing laundry in my apartment one weekend, and I was stopped in my tracks by a thought. God had been impressing on me that I was a treasure, and that I wasn't to settle for a man who treated me as anything less than that. To see that idea represented visually at the moment God created my life was nothing short of amazing for me. As Ellen led me through my nine months in the womb, I saw Jesus cradling me the entire time. I was supported and protected by Him even before I had entered the world. Just before I heard Ellen talking about me having a heartbeat, I saw Jesus lift me to His lips and kiss me gently, blessing me with life.

As I was being born, I sensed Him right there with me, saying, "Don't be afraid." He was my source of strength, courage, and peace from the very beginning of my life. As I took my first breath, I knew it was God breathing His life into my lungs. I sensed His pleasure in me, the same pleasure He must have known as He breathed life into Adam and declared His creation "very good." I saw Jesus holding me after I was born. He raised His hand to His lips, kissed it, and then placed it on my forehead like a seal of approval. His touch was gentle, kind, loving, and incredibly tender. As He was cradling me in His arms, I saw His stance change a bit. He was holding me in His right arm, and His left was extended out with His palm up in a "stop" motion. The message I sensed was clear, "This one is Mine. She belongs to Me. Nothing will come near and harm her. She is protected and safe in My arms."

At this point, Ellen asked if I wanted to hold the newborn me. Part of me thought I should say yes because that seemed like the right answer, but the truth was that I didn't want to do it. When I declined, Ellen asked me about my reluctance. I'd never been comfortable around babies, and it was no different even in the visualization exercise. I just always felt detached when it came to new life and never chose to engage with it. Eventually, though, I grew curious and brave enough to reach out and accept the infant version of myself into my arms. I marveled at the perfection of God's handiwork—a newborn child, totally healthy, all pink and full of life, peacefully cooing, and moving her arms and legs about, as if trying to figure out how they worked. I'd never seen myself as beautiful in that way. I just kept staring at my infant self, realizing for the first time how magnificent a gift life is, and how incomprehensible our God becomes in light of this creative power. Ellen then asked me if there was anything I wanted to say to the child, perhaps in the form of speaking a blessing over her. I hesitated for a few seconds, then spoke what came to mind, including "peace and joy, great strength (more than you realize), confidence, protected, a warrior princess, and perfectly made." As soon as I had finished speaking the blessing, the infant version of me dissolved like smoke and entered me, becoming not just a *part* of me, but becoming an entirely new me.

The last visual I saw in the exercise was Jesus setting me on the ground. I was a young girl, able to walk on my own. He took my hand and we stood there together, ready to head off into a great adventure. As Ellen wrapped up the exercise and closed us in prayer,

I felt peaceful and loved in a way I'd never known. I'd been so afraid before, even afraid of my infant self. I'd been hesitant to embrace who God had shown me I was, but as I took in that truth and let it sink deep into every part of me, it began to change me from the inside out. God's love began to replace my fear and give me courage and no longer did I feel like an accident.

Before I left that appointment, Ellen told me that it was time to spread out my elbows and take up some room in this world. God had been intentional about creating me and it was ok for me to be here. My value didn't exist in what I could do for others. My purpose wasn't rooted in completing another person. My meaning in life wasn't tied to any particular role or title I held. I mattered because God made me. My opinions, feelings, thoughts, ideas, knowledge, skills, and gifting were important because God gave them to me. It was ok to share those things with the world, and I no longer had to hide who I was or be a chameleon. I no longer had to apologize for how God had designed me.

Those truths were the beginning of healthy boundaries for me, but there was still more work to be done. As we continued with my counseling, we began tackling old lies, agreements, and unhealthy soul ties — specifically, we began to clean up my sexual past.

Going through the rebirthing exercise was just one step in correcting how I saw myself. I still had a lot of baggage to unload from the years I spent sleeping around with men, seeking love and self-worth in all the wrong places. In August 2012, I made the following entry in my journal: *I'm not happy about how I relate to men. I immediately look to see if they are married, and I relate to them in terms of their potential as a partner. I hate it. It brings up feelings of desperation and immaturity, like my worth and value are in whether or not they find me attractive.* A couple of days later, Ellen sent a text message with the name of a book. She suggested I read *The Invisible Bond* by Barbara Wilson.[14] In the book, Wilson explains how God wired us for physical intimacy within the context of marriage, and why sex outside of marriage is so damaging. As I read through the book, I saw so much of myself in those pages. Through the study questions, God began to reveal the messages I had picked up from my parents about love, sex, and marriage and He showed me how those messages had contributed to my behavior later on in life.

As I worked through the book, Ellen and I started tackling the lies I'd believed and agreements I'd made. Maybe some of these statements will sound familiar in your own life: I'll always have to settle; I'm not worthy of anything or anyone really good or special; My dreams are never going to come true; I'd be better off alone in life; I have to take care of myself, protect myself, provide for myself because no one else will (including God); My mistakes will destroy me; I'll never have another relationship as good as the one I had with (fill in the blank); No one can be trusted except for God; I'll never be worthy to be the "real" girlfriend; I'll never be good enough, attractive enough, or interesting enough; My only worth is in my sexuality; I will always have to be the one who does the pursuing in dating.

One by one, we renounced those lies and agreements and we replaced them with God's truth. A month later, we went through the exercise of breaking the soul ties I'd accumulated during my years of promiscuity. It turned out to be harder than I thought. As Ellen led me through a prayer to break all connections with those men, she asked me to list each one of them by name. Let me tell you, it's one thing to see the names written on a sheet of paper, but it's another thing entirely to speak those names out loud. I wasn't prepared for the feelings of shame and embarrassment that surfaced while I read through my list and confessed my sin in this area.

That's why we are so reluctant to confess our sins to God. We want to hold on to them and keep them in the dark. We don't want to engage with our holy and righteous God because in His presence, we see our sin as He does. God hates sin and so should we, but the Bible says that if we confess our sins, God is faithful to forgive us and cleanse us from all unrighteousness.[15] Confession clears the air between us and God. Sin gets in the way of intimacy, and that's why the enemy loves to push our shame button. He doesn't want us to be close and intimate with God. He doesn't want us to confess, but as painful as it can sometimes be, confessing is exactly what we need to do.

The second time Ellen asked me to read through the list of names, it was to break the ties and separate myself completely from those men. It was a bit easier to read the list that time, knowing I was clearing the past and moving forward free of all that baggage. When we finished, I felt significantly lighter. Often, we don't realize the weight of our past until we deal with it and let it go.

It was during this same time that I was working through yet another aspect of sexual sin with God. I wasn't sleeping with anyone, but I hadn't yet given up the habit of satisfying my own desires. Masturbation is one of those sins that we easily justify because it doesn't seem to hurt anyone. It seems like a harmless pursuit and doesn't seem sinful. I spent a long time questioning God about it, asking him if it really was a sin, and why it was. I even did my own research online to see if I could get a clear answer, but none of the sites I visited brought any resolution for me. One day, though, I heard a sermon about sex outside of marriage and the pastor explained how we make our bed an altar when we worship the god of our flesh — and that included worshipping *our own flesh.* Simply put, it was idolatry.

I'd never thought about it that way, quite frankly, but it was exactly what I needed to hear. Additionally, God put some Bible verses front and center in my reading. 1 Corinthians 6:19 reads:

> *Or do you not know that **your body is a temple** of the Holy Spirit who is in you, whom you have from God, and that you are not your own? For you have been bought with a price; therefore glorify God in your body.* (emphasis mine)

And 1 Corinthians 3:16-17 says this about our body:

> *Do you not know that you are a temple of God and that the Spirit of God dwells in you? If any man*

destroys the temple of God, God will destroy him,
**for the temple of God is holy, and that is what
you are**. (emphasis mine)

Those pieces of Scripture completely changed my
perspective about my body. God was telling me in
His Word that my body was holy ground. I may not
have been worshipping the flesh with another person,
but I was still worshipping and setting the pleasure
of my own flesh above God. By His grace and with
the power of the Holy Spirit, I was able to stop my
old behaviors and start treating myself in healthier,
more respectful ways. As God helped me put to death
all of the areas of sexual sin in my life, I began to see
others, as well as myself, in a whole new way. Sexual
fantasies and daydreams became almost non-existent.
Interestingly, once I stopped idolizing my own body,
my thoughts about men began to change as well. Over
the next two years, God would bring several men into
my life in platonic roles. Through those men and their
friendships, God would provide safe environments
for me to work out personal boundaries and define
preferences for a future spouse. I would learn to practice wisdom and discernment as I evaluated charac-
teristics and behaviors against the measuring stick of
God's Word.

Chapter 21

DON'T WANNA, NOT GONNA, CAN'T MAKE ME

The word of the Lord came to Jonah the son of Amittai saying, "Arise, go to Nineveh the great city and cry against it, for their wickedness has come up before Me." But Jonah rose up to flee to Tarshish from the presence of the Lord. So he went down to Joppa, found a ship which was going to Tarshish, paid the fare and went down into it to go with them to Tarshish from the presence of the Lord. – **Jonah 1:1-3**

In the spring of 2012, I was approaching the end of my Rocklin apartment lease, and was desperately trying to find a room to rent in the Folsom area. I began sharing with a few friends, asking around for rental opportunities. I followed up on a few leads but nothing panned out. Every door I pushed on would end up closing and closing tight. The only door that seemed to be wide open was the one leading me to more time in Orange County, and I was adamantly opposed to that option. Folsom was familiar. I loved the neighborhoods and I loved the weather. Most of my friends lived there and my home church was there. I saw no reason to move, but the clock was ticking and I was no closer to finding a room to rent in Folsom.

About six weeks before the end of my lease, I began feeling pressure in my relationship with God. I'm talking about physical pressure, like I was being squeezed from all around, and one phrase kept running through my mind: "You're being resistant." I knew God was pointing me in the direction of Southern California, but I just didn't want to look at that option. I saw Him holding that door open, but I figured if I ignored it long and hard enough, that God would take pity on me and open a door in Folsom. Instead, the voice in my head grew more insistent: "You're being resistant." Pretty soon, the word "resistant" was replaced with "disobedient". God was calling me out and I had no place to hide. I felt the physical pressure, but I was also growing tired mentally; try as I might, I couldn't keep ignoring God's prompting. He is a force to be reckoned with, and anyone who has ever tried to oppose Him has lost in spectacular fashion.

I was so much like Jonah during this time. I saw Southern California like Jonah saw Nineveh. I couldn't imagine a worse place to be sent and I absolutely didn't want to go. In my own way, I was running from God's will as much as Jonah. I couldn't see past my own desires, and couldn't begin to imagine why it was so important to God to take me away from my friends and family. I was in the midst of the annulment process. I was neck-deep in my counseling issues. Why on earth would God take me out of my comfort zone in the middle of all that? Why would He essentially make me homeless, splitting my time between two part-time residences? Why would He take away that one last vestige of comfort and security?

One day, I finally caved in, sort of. I told God, "Ok, Lord, I'm willing to talk about what it might look like *if* I were to agree to go to Orange County." I'd been telling friends and family for months that I didn't want to be in Southern California full-time. Agreeing to simply discuss the option with God felt like a monumental concession on my part, and I believe God understood that. The pressure immediately vanished and God graciously imparted His plan. I didn't have to find a place full-time down south. I could simply flip my current schedule and spend three weeks every month in Orange County and one week in Northern California. I asked friends to pray with me as I asked God for a greater willingness to embrace what He was showing me and for Him to work out all the details if this truly was His plan.

God wasted no time revealing His provision for my move down south. He opened the hearts of my sister and brother-in-law so that I could stay with them during my one week up north each month. He did the same with my coworker in Orange County. She agreed to house me for three weeks at a time, and she was willing to do it rent-free to help me pay down my debt. God gave me favor with my supervisor, who was thrilled at the idea of having me down south most of the time, and He even arranged approval for a mileage stipend to pay for my expenses to drive back and forth between Orange County and Northern California each month.

I didn't understand what God was doing, but I couldn't deny where and how He was leading. It was time to stop asking questions, and start trusting and obeying. My faith was small, my trust was reluctant, and my obedience was sloppy. My leap of faith in that season looked less like a leap and more like I was getting kicked off a steep cliff. Nevertheless, off I went to

Southern California. I felt like I was being exiled, and in a way I was. But that, I discovered, is when God does some of His best work.

As I entered that season, I came across this verse from 1 Kings 17:2-4:

> *The word of the Lord came to him (Elijah), saying, 'Go away from here and turn eastward, and hide yourself by the brook Cherith, which is east of the Jordan. It shall be that you will drink of the brook, and I have commanded the ravens to provide for you there.'*

I felt very much like Elijah, in that I had no idea what lay ahead in the wilderness, but I knew that God was good. There would be many days in the next two years where that particular truth would be all I could grasp. Knowing that God was always good despite the reality of my circumstances would get me through workplace challenges, lonely days, and countless moments where I just wanted to throw up my hands and quit. It would be my prayer in moments of extreme frustration as I confessed that He was good and that I could trust in Him when I could trust in no one or nothing else around me. I would learn, as Elijah did, that God is completely trustworthy in the wilderness, that He nourishes His children in the desert, and that a season of stillness and solitude with God is sometimes necessary to prepare us for our next assignment.

While Elijah was sent directly into the desert, God was kind enough to allow me a transition period as I entered my own wilderness season. He didn't force me to go cold turkey and immediately move to Orange County full-time. For the last seven months of 2012, I split my time between Northern and Southern California; when things got a little too squirrelly for my liking down south, I knew that I only had to wait a couple of weeks before I got to go home and spend a week recharging my battery.

As I began my season in Orange County, my coworker began spending more time away from the office. Her husband had been diagnosed with Stage 4 pancreatic cancer at the beginning of the year, and she was needed at home to help take care of him along with their four children. I could not have foreseen this turn of events, but God certainly did. He knew that she would need distraction-free time with her family without worrying that she was leaving her coworkers in a bind. You see, God never moves us just for our own benefit. We may get what we're praying for, but it's never so that we can go merrily on our way, living for ourselves. God always has a greater purpose, and it always involves other people. God saw that my coworker would need this time away from work, and His solution was to put me in Orange County to fill in the gap. Her husband would eventually lose his fight with cancer in November, and she would end up taking an extended absence in early 2013, but God had a plan for that, too.

As I got ready to go back up to Northern California in December for a two-week vacation, I felt God prompting me to stop making trips up north. The drive had started to feel like more of a hassle, and each trip found me looking forward to it less and less. On top of that, my sister had told me in early December that she and her husband had decided to short sell their home. I'd gone through so much transition the previous two years that I really couldn't stomach the thought of yet another change, especially if it meant navigating a move long-distance. By the time I made it up at Christmas, I was convinced it would be my last trip for a while.

When I got to my sister's that December, I found that the guest bathroom, which was always cleaned up in anticipation of my stay, was a disaster area. In fact, it looked like all of my stuff had been moved out of the way and they had moved their own stuff back into it. Granted, I had told them that I would be housesitting at a friend's during my stay, but there was still an overwhelming feeling that I was being told my time there was over. When I went back to their house for Christmas Eve dinner, I spent the time after dinner packing up the remainder of my things, and told my sister and brother-in-law that I wasn't going to make any more trips up north; I felt like I needed to be down south full-time at that point. God had given me seven months to adjust to my new surroundings, and in His grace I finally felt like I was ready to camp out by the brook without running back home every few weeks.

I never had a desire to work in accounting, banking, or information technology; I don't have a gifting for any of those fields and I don't have a strong interest in them, either. Yet that's exactly where I ended up after I returned from Washington and was rehired by my former employer. That's where they had a vacancy, and that's where I was placed. Before long, I was tackling help desk tickets submitted for our company's primary software program, many of which were for the accounting modules. I was also tasked with backing up my coworker in a number of banking functions within the program. Needless to say, my learning curve when I joined that department was pretty high. When I'd worked with the company previously, I'd learned the software but it was on the management side of the house, not accounting. There was also no formal training program in place, so I learned nearly everything I needed to know on the fly. That's a stressful way to learn, especially when you're not crazy about the type of work in the first place.

Technology itself is a temperamental beast. One day, everything is working fine; the next, all you-know-what is breaking loose. One small change to the software code can set off a chain reaction of issues, and before you know it, you're inundated with help desk tickets, calls, and emails from users who suddenly can't do their job. Click the wrong button and you've credited someone's account instead of debiting it. Select the wrong option and you could accidentally delete a record. Poke around in the wrong part of the database and you could update a collection of records with the wrong information. It was so easy to make a mistake, and so painful to correct it. It was frustrating and tense work for me. My coworker had no fear when it came to clicking buttons and trying things out. I, on the other hand, had to spend several minutes screwing up the courage to attempt something new for fear of starting one of those dreaded chain reactions. I had no faith in my own abilities, and I had no faith in the system. Even though I knew that the data was being backed up every few minutes, I didn't trust that a catastrophic mistake could be remedied with a data restore command.

During this season, I was literally at the mercy of God to get me through my days. I needed God's help to learn the systems and programs and to reveal solutions to problems. I needed His grace to give me the right attitude to serve others in the workplace. When circumstances became uncomfortable, frightening, and stressful, I needed His help to persevere. Most of all, I needed God's help to be honest about how I felt in my moments of weakness.

Self-sufficiency is one of the many masks we tend to wear in this life that keeps us from enjoying intimacy with God. We start to think that we can handle our circumstances without Him. We start to live and work in our own power. We gloss over the challenges and difficulties we are facing, and we minimize how we feel about them. We beat ourselves up and shame ourselves into trying harder; at least, that's how I usually responded. I mistakenly believed that it was how God wanted me to respond. I bought into the lie that

God helps those who help themselves, but the truth is that God helps those who *cannot* help themselves, and are brave — and humble enough — to admit it.

That's where I found myself on numerous occasions during this season at work. Moments of brutal honesty with God happened at all hours and in all locations: on the drive to work, on the drive home from work, in the ladies' room, lying in bed, sitting at my desk, and in the middle of meetings. The drives home were usually filled with the greatest venting as I unloaded my day to God. I remember one conversation in particular. It had been an especially frantic day. Everything had blown up first thing in the morning, and the remainder of the day had been spent trying to put the pieces back together. It was like running a cliff edge with little bombs going off while you try to not lose your footing and tumble down the hillside. By the time I got in my car, I was toast and I wasted no time in letting God know it. When I finished, His response seemed to be, "But everything got resolved, yes?" I sat there for a moment, knowing He was right, but reluctant to admit it. After a few deep breaths, I replied, "Yes, yes they did." A heartbeat later, I continued, "But, You are totally missing my point here! I'm not happy about how it all went down!" The issues *had* been resolved, but the last minute timing of it all had left me exhausted and wrung out. I wasn't happy about following God along that cliff edge. I didn't understand why we couldn't have taken a safer and more comfortable route to the same destination.

At that point in the conversation, I would have expected God to be upset with me, but He wasn't. Instead, I sensed Him smiling at me and I felt loved. We try so hard to be good for God, but what He really wants is for us to be authentic. He died so we could have a relationship with Him, not so that we could spend the rest of our life *pretending* to have a relationship with Him. Self-sufficiency prevents God's grace from being enough. It's why we read in 2 Corinthians 12:9 that God's grace is sufficient, and that His power and strength are perfected in our weakness. It is only when we come to Him, willing to admit that we can no longer handle things, that His grace can take over and become more than enough in our circumstances and in our life.

Often, we don't see God's breaking work in us as something to rejoice over. Instead, we whine and complain about how hard a season is for us. It's so easy to lose sight of the goal, that of God's constant sanctification. We overlook the fact that the daily process is the end result; in God's economy, the journey really *is* the destination. The daily choices we make to trust, to obey, to endure and persevere, and to praise God even when we don't understand or like what's happening — they are the fruit of a sanctified life. Because of that, we can do as Psalm 51:8 encourages and we can let the bones which God has broken rejoice. Sanctification doesn't always feel good, but it *is* good. It is good of God to not leave us in our current condition, and it is good of Him to help us along to a more mature place in our relationship with Him.

Chapter 22

STILLNESS AND SOLITUDE

Be still (cease striving) and know that I am God.
– Psalm 46:10

Stillness and solitude aren't things that come very naturally to us as human beings. The only time we seem to do it well is when we sleep. It seems to me an act of extreme grace that God created us with physical limitations, requiring us to stop and sleep. While it may not feel like it at the time, seasons of forced stillness and solitude are also the actions of a gracious God. It may be for purposes of rest and recuperation. It may be for teaching and preparation. Or, it may be an opportunity to practice the things our heavenly Father has taught us. Whatever the obvious reason, the greater underlying purpose is always a deeper communion with God.

When the Lord told Elijah to go and hide himself by the brook, it was to nourish and prepare him for the next season and assignments. When God delivered the Israelites out of slavery in Egypt and into the wilderness, it was to prepare them to receive the Promised Land and all that it contained. When the Holy Spirit led Jesus into the wilderness for 40 days, it was to test and prepare Him for His ministry. In all three circumstances, each person or group was taken away from what was familiar and comfortable for them. In each case, they were completely dependent upon God and His presence, power, and provision. There was no one except God to feed Elijah in the desert. There was no one except God to sustain and lead the Israelites in the wilderness. There was no one except God to protect Jesus in the desert. Each of these experiences presented opportunities to call upon God and draw closer to Him.

God talks about drawing us close to Him in the wilderness in Hosea 2:14-16:

"Therefore, behold, I will allure her, bring her into the wilderness and speak kindly to her. Then I will give her her vineyards from there, and the valley of

Achor as a door of hope. And she will sing there as in
the days of her youth, as in the day when she came
up from the land of Egypt. It will come about in that
day," declares the Lord, "that you will call Me Ishi
(Husband) and will no longer call Me Baali (Master)."

I'm especially fond of the last verse. It illustrates
the transition we make in our relationship with God
during seasons in the wilderness. We move from a
more formal and detached relationship of Master
and servant to one that's far more intimate — that of a
bride and Groom.

The Bible says that God is jealous for us. He desires
fidelity and commitment in our relationship with
Him, and one way to grow that is for us to first experience *His* faithfulness and commitment towards us.
Oftentimes, though, the only way for us to do that is
to be whisked away from our daily routines and have
our lives disrupted in such a way that we become
hyper-aware of everything, including God's still small
voice. Elijah himself learned that God wasn't in the
loud and explosive things like fire, earthquakes, and
a mighty wind. Rather, God revealed Himself to Elijah
in a gentle whisper.[16] Why a whisper, you might ask?

If you've ever spent time in the desert, you know
how quiet it can be. There isn't much in the desert

to distract you. The wilderness, in its own austere way, forces us to become silent and still. It is the perfect environment in which to meditate on God and His Word, and to hear from Him. In the wilderness, there's no reason to shout. Any little sound will carry, and in that kind of season, our attention to God and His whispers is sharpened.

But that's not the main reason God whispers; He does it because He is close. It is in the desert seasons when we sometimes feel most alone, but that is exactly when God is the closest to us. When God moved me to Orange County, I felt very alone because my friends and family were all up north. I'd finished 15 months of counseling and wasn't making any more trips to Folsom to see my therapist. I didn't have a home church down south yet, so I had no small group or accountability partners. It was just me and God. When I was frustrated, I vented to God. When I was sad, I cried to God. When I was lonely, I talked with God. When I failed, I confessed to God. When I was confused, I questioned God. When things went well, I praised God. And when I wanted to give up, I opened God's Word for hope and encouragement. I can't tell you how many times I came home from work in tears, begging God for encouragement to persevere, only to open His Word and read the very thing I most needed.

In the desert, God broke down my self-sufficiency, and He and His grace became all-sufficient. In the wilderness, I learned how to get still before God and hear His voice. Exile can feel like punishment, but I learned that it's a gift. Look at these words from Jeremiah 31:2-3 as God talks about His people, Israel:

> *Thus says the Lord, "The people who survived the sword found grace in the wilderness – Israel, when it went to find its rest." The Lord appeared to me from afar, saying, "I have loved you with an everlasting love; therefore I have drawn you with lovingkindness."*

God draws us into the desert out of a heart of love in order to show us grace – it is a great kindness to be called out and into the singular presence of our God.

In our lifetime, most of us will never serve in a high profile capacity for God. Most of us will serve in obscurity, influencing only the immediate community where God has placed us. We will be legends in our own minds and famous only to those closest to us. Because of that, we may be tempted to think that we aren't having much of an impact on God's kingdom, but we would be wrong.

We cannot see the entire plan that God has laid out for the world or the impact we are having on people around us when we obey Him. We might have a conversation with someone about our faith, only to be rejected, unaware that our words were planting seeds in the heart of another person who was listening in on the conversation. A seemingly insignificant act of kindness might be witnessed by a stranger whose heart is softened just enough for God to gain a foothold and lead them to a saving faith in Jesus, thereby altering their eternal future. The implications of our trust and obedience are greater than we can imagine.

It's easy to place serving or ministry in a box of our own making, believing that it has to look a certain way in order to qualify as pleasing to God. I know because I've done it on many an occasion. When I was living in Folsom, I would have classified much of how I spent my free time as "serving" or "ministry". I met with women from church over coffee and spent time encouraging them and coming alongside them in prayer. I was serving in several capacities within my church and in the community. I felt useful to God and didn't doubt my role as a servant in God's kingdom.

Soon after being sidelined by my prodigal detour in Washington State, and entering a season of stillness and solitude, I began to experience bouts of feeling useless. I began to wonder if I would ever be used by God again, especially in any significant capacity. Despite my constant prayers about it, God remained silent when it came to finding a home church in Orange County; consequently, I wasn't serving in any kind of official ministry role. Little did I know that God was, in fact, using me. I didn't recognize it at first because it didn't look like any kind of serving I had done in the past. In Folsom, serving was compartmentalized, something I did apart from my home and work life, but in bringing me down to Orange County, God turned my home and work life into service. Despite the lack of a home church and specific ministry, I was still serving.

Simply showing up to work each day was meeting a need for my coworker whose husband was battling pancreatic cancer. She missed a lot of work during the first year I rejoined the company, and my presence in the office allowed her the freedom to minister to her family in their time of need, both before and after his death. My home life became service, as well. My roommate had Multiple Sclerosis and was wheelchair-bound. God gave me the opportunity to help with caregiving tasks and generally just help make my roommate's life a bit easier.

I never would have chosen to serve in these capacities, but in obeying God's leading to move to Orange County, I entered into a life of service instead of just occasionally serving in a formal ministry. Over time, it radically changed my thinking as I lived out Romans 12:1:

> *Therefore I urge you, brethren, by the mercies of God, to present your bodies a living and holy sacrifice, acceptable to God, which is your spiritual service of worship.*

Service isn't something God calls us to do; it's the life He calls us to live — every day and everywhere.

In following God down to Orange County, I gave up my own desires, hopes, wishes, and dreams. I surrendered my will to His. In a very small way, relative to Jesus' submission to the Father, I had been invited into communion with Christ and His obedience. In order to fully appreciate the blessings that Jesus enjoyed, it's important to first align ourselves and understand His surrender and suffering. In fact, I would suggest that it's impossible to truly embrace and experience the joys of God's blessing until we have been stripped as Jesus was, and until we have suffered as He did.

Jesus was stripped of many things the day He was crucified. He was stripped of His clothing. He was stripped of His dignity. He was stripped of His comfort. He was even stripped of flesh and bone during His scourging. All these things were torn from Him and He was left bare and exposed before God and before men. In our own life, that stripping can take any number of forms. We can be stripped of position and power. We can be stripped of identity. We can be stripped of possessions. We can be stripped of physical, emotional, or financial health. Whatever the circumstances, the stripping away and crucifixion of self are never pleasant—and yet, they are an essential piece of the Christian experience.

Had Christ not been obedient to death on a cross, there would have been no resurrection victory. There would have been no Lamb of God to take away our sin, no one upon whom the Father could have poured out the full measure of His wrath. In His death and resurrection, Jesus demonstrated the truth of what He told His disciples in John 12:24: "…unless a grain of wheat falls into the earth and dies, it remains alone; but if it dies, it bears much fruit." In Jesus' death and resurrection, He made a way for *all* mankind to be saved and to experience eternal life with God.

Our obedience usually does not have such widespread or grand consequences, but that's not the point. God's ultimate goal for each of us is to be more like Jesus. We are to learn how to take up our cross each day and carry it for God's glory. We are to grow in grace as the things of self and the world are removed from our life. We are to sharpen our gaze upon that which is eternal and unseen. We are to practice laying down our life each day as we allow God to use our time and talents to advance His kingdom agenda. Through it all, we join with Christ in experiencing and managing the tension of the Garden of Gethsemane.

Knowing that He was about to enter His final hours on earth, Jesus' prayer in the garden illustrates the struggle we all face in obeying God. In Matthew 26:39, we read Jesus' plea, "My Father, if it is possible, let this cup pass from Me; yet not as I will, but as You will." Jesus wasn't a masochist. He wasn't looking forward to suffering and dying on a cross. In fact, in the verse just before His prayer, we read that Jesus told His disciples that He was exceedingly sorrowful. That word for sorrowful comes from two words: one meaning sadness and the other meaning thorough or complete, the root of which means to pierce or go through. In other words, Jesus was totally consumed with sadness or sorrow at the prospect of His suffering, to the point that He actually began to sweat drops of blood. Where do you think we got the term "sweating blood"?

And the word "excruciating"? It comes from the Latin word crux, meaning cross. The word *excruciare* means to thoroughly cause pain or anguish. It literally means "to crucify." When we struggle in our obedience, we join Jesus in the garden. When we surrender and obey, we join Jesus on the cross. In this process, we experience the reality of Hebrews 12:2 which tells us that "for the joy set before Him, (Jesus) endured the cross." We might understand this joy in an abstract way like I did for a long time, but when we regularly practice surrender, that joy is grown in our heart and becomes a deep-seated reality in our life.

In my first three years as a Christian, I was only too happy to share in Jesus' blessings. Life was good and easy, but I knew neither the pain nor the joy of Jesus. I had not yet been crucified with Christ. I had not yet known what it was like to really lay down my life for another. During my time in Southern California, I was given the chance to practice and experience all of those things. Everything I'd known and been was torn from me, one painful piece at a time. Every time I thought we were done, God would show me yet one more attitude, perception, lie, creature comfort, or relationship that He wanted to take away. "How much more?" I would cry. "How much more do I have to give up?" There were days when I was so angry about all that I'd lost. Some days, I literally felt like I was on the floor, raw and bleeding, vulnerable and exposed. I would call to mind the verse from Psalm 30:5 about weeping lasting for a night and joy arriving with a shout in the morning. I would meditate on Hebrews 12:2 and cling to the promise that there was joy yet unseen set before me. I would beg God, as David did in Psalm 143:8, to reveal His unfailing lovingkindness in the morning as I entrusted my soul to Him.

Those verses gave me hope. They gave me the strength to keep going and to be still in the suffering. I can't tell you how many times I wanted to quit. I wanted to look for another job. I wanted to find a place of my own to live. I wanted to move back to Folsom or Washington State. I wanted to give up on my debt repayment plan and go back to my old habits. I wanted to be anywhere except where I was, but with every choice I made to remain, I entered into an indescribable place of union with Christ and walked out the truth of Galatians 2:20, *"I have been crucified with Christ and it is no longer I who live, but Christ lives in me..."* As I continually let go of things like striving, self-sufficiency, and leaning on my own understanding — as I committed to joining Jesus in the garden — I began to know His peace that surpasses all understanding, His love that casts out all fear, and His power that moves mountains. I finally began to know Christ, and not just know *about* Him.

Chapter 23

FREEDOM

It was for freedom that Christ set us free; therefore keep standing firm and do not be subject again to a yoke of slavery. – **Galatians 5:1**

F reedom — people have fought and died for it. Some people only dream of it. Some of us take for granted the abundance of it that we have always known. Still others never fully take advantage of it. Saddest of all are those who relinquish it because the weight and responsibility of it are simply too great to bear.

When freedom is easily achieved, it is often not appreciated. In the same vein, when freedom is something you have always known, it is often not appreciated until it is lost, stolen, or squandered. When God freed the Israelites from Egyptian bondage, He didn't immediately place them in the Promised Land. He led them through the desert first, but it wasn't to punish them; it was to prepare them.

For 400 years, they had lived as slaves without the presence of God among them. They didn't know how to be in relationship with God. The same could be said of me after my return from Washington. I knew about God, and I had a distant type of relationship with Him, but I didn't really know how to do life with Him day in and day out. Like the Israelites, I had to be prepared for freedom. I needed a wilderness season of intimacy with God to learn what He was really like and to experience Him in a personal way. I needed to practice relating to Him, trusting Him, believing Him, and obeying Him. For me, much of that practice happened as God led me into financial freedom.

It was a long-fought, hard-won battle that started with the poor example I inherited from my parents. As a kid, I watched them use every credit card known to man to live life beyond their means, surviving from paycheck to paycheck. As soon as I had held down a job for a year, I applied for a collection of credit cards: Visa, MasterCard, and a fistful of retail store cards. I quickly charged each one to its limit and began to live as my parents had, making only the minimum monthly payments and always hovering near the limits on my accounts. The idea of savings accounts and living on a budget never entered my thinking. My fiscal household was built on a foundation of folly, and it showed in the decisions I made. One of my more ridiculous escapades involved securing a $3,000 loan for someone I was casually dating — though even that was an overstatement of the relationship — because he was having trouble meeting his financial obligations. Needless to say, that arrangement didn't turn out well, though the loan eventually was paid off.

A few years later, when I left my job with the State of California, I cashed out my small collection of tax-sheltered annuities and paid off the debt I had accumulated up until that time. In one fell swoop, I was debt-free, for less than a year. I eventually applied for a credit card and I soon maxed it out. One card turned into two, and the cycle began all over again. Pretty soon, I had enough debt going that I was transferring balances left and right onto new credit cards and lines of credit with zero interest introductory rates to keep the interest at bay.

One night, about two years after becoming a Christian, I began to think about my finances as I was listening to some praise and worship music. I was desperate to be free of my bills and I was exhausted from carrying the burden myself. I knew it was time to face my debt head-on and talk with God openly and honestly about it. On my knees, alone in my apartment, I confessed my lifetime of foolish decisions. I admitted my inability to manage my money well and told God I knew it wasn't pleasing or honoring to Him to steward my finances the way that I had. Then I surrendered my will to His: "Lord, I know that You are able to take away this debt load, and I desperately want You to. But if there's a greater purpose in me continuing to carry this load, then so be it. I'm going to trust You to take care of me and provide for me." As I finished that prayer, the opening notes to Chris Tomlin's "My Deliverer" began to play, and I began to cry. To this day, I cannot tell you how I knew it, but I knew in that moment that God was promising to deliver me from my debt. I didn't know how and I didn't know when, but I was absolutely certain that He would make good on His promise and that was good enough. Going forward, even though my financial condition hadn't changed, the weight of it was noticeably lighter.

The following year, I met my third husband. He told me that his finances were in good shape, that he was making plenty of money, and that once I moved up to Washington, I wouldn't have to work. Best of all, he would help me pay off my bills. *God was making good on His promise*, I thought. Unfortunately, as I wrote earlier, Paul's financial situation wasn't quite as rosy as he'd led me to believe. My dream of an easy life and a free ticket into financial freedom died with that marriage, and I entered 2012 alone and still living under the weight of $25,000 of personal debt.

As that year began, I found myself haunted by a recurring thought: *I have to get out of debt.* It was no longer an idle desire; the thought pursued me day in and day out, and it brought along friends. *Your debt is preventing God from using you like He intends. Your debt load is a hindrance. It's a roadblock to the next things God has for you.* As the lease to my Rocklin apartment came to a close in May 2012, I decided I was ready to act on things — and God was ready to step in and start providing.

He opened my coworker's heart and she opened her home to me, as did my sister and brother-in-law. I was able to live rent-free and redirect those funds toward my debt load. God gave me favor at work, and enabled me to grow and prosper in a new role within my company. He took care of my then 11-year-old car and kept it running so I wouldn't have to make any major repairs. And for 16 months, God gave me the

grace to persevere through moment after moment of
just wanting to quit.

December 2012 was the toughest month. It was
roughly the halfway point in my journey, and that's
always where the rubber meets the road. You're past
the starting point and the novelty of the journey has
long worn off, and you're too far from the finish line
to get excited about sprinting to the end. You're just in
the middle, no-man's-land, and ripe for the enemy's
temptations. That month, I got a wild hair to buy a
ring for myself, some symbol of my relationship with
God. I bought, and returned, four rings that month.
It was only by God's amazing grace that I exited that
month without backsliding into deeper debt.

The middle of the journey is also the toughest
place to take a step of faith. It was around this time
that I reworked my budget after having paid off three
of my five credit card accounts. As I ran the numbers, I realized that I would see an increase of about
$1,000 each month once I was debt-free. I committed
to increase my tithe by $100 once that happened, but
then felt like God was prompting me to take that step
right then as an act of faith. That same week, I listened
to a sermon at New Song where my pastor encouraged the congregation to increase their giving by $100
each month. That was all the confirmation I needed,

and I took the leap. Looking back, I have no doubt that my obedience in this area contributed to the enemy's efforts to derail me in December.

In February 2013, I found out that I was going to owe $2,000 in federal and state taxes. I had been slated to finish paying things off in June, but the unexpected tax debt quickly changed all that. After praying and considering my options, I did what I hoped was the wisest thing under the circumstances. I took advantage of a promotional offer with one of the cards I had not yet paid off and got the funds I needed at a 0% interest rate. As I adjusted my new completion date to September, Proverbs 13:12 took on a whole new meaning: "Hope deferred makes the heart sick..." Nevertheless, I chose to believe God was working things out beyond what I could see and that we *would* finish the journey.

On September 20, 2013, I crossed that finish line and God made good on His promise. It was a quieter and more subdued victory than I had imagined. No ticker tape. No bands playing. No fanfare. In fact, it took several months simply for the magnitude of the accomplishment to even sink in. I was in awe of what God had done. It's true that we did it together, but it's also true that we did not. God did all the heavy lifting; I really just followed along after Him, watching Him work. He gets all the glory and all the celebration because I simply could not have done it without Him. If I could have, I would have. The truth is that I wasn't capable of doing it in my own power, any more than I was capable of saving myself without the work that Jesus did for me on the cross.

Freedom. For years, I only dreamt of it. When I had it briefly, I took it for granted. I didn't fully leverage it for something greater than myself. For 16 months, I fought for it and died to myself in order to obtain it. After achieving that freedom, my prayer was that I would not relinquish it. My prayer was that God would equip me to steward well the weight and responsibility of that freedom, to His glory and the advancement of His Kingdom. A couple of months later, God put me in a spiritual disciplines class which included a section on financial stewardship and budgeting. For the first time in my life, I drafted a budget and by the grace of God, I've been adhering to it ever since.

Freedom is never free; neither is wellness. Both require that something or someone pay a price. Something or someone usually has to die. When it comes to freedom, it could be a perception, an attitude, a way of life, a behavior, an idea, a condition, a habit, a custom, a rule or law, a government, or a soldier. When it comes to healing and wellness, it could be a part of our identity, or it could be an individual, as in the person of Jesus Christ dying for our sins. Whatever it is, something old has to give way to make room for something new.

You've heard it said that a body in motion tends to stay in motion, and a body at rest tends to stay at rest. The same is true for our old mindsets and behaviors. The ideas and habits that have existed within us all of our life tend to be set, and it requires significant effort to change them. It's far easier to continue along in the same patterns than to try and break new ground. Sticking to our old ways is also safe, comfortable, and familiar. Our life may not be all that we want it to be, or all that we know it could be, but at least we understand it and know how to relate to it. It's predictable.

Freedom and wellness require that we move out of our comfort zone into unknown territory. It requires effort and courage. It requires that the pain and discomfort of our current situation outweigh the fear of the unknown, new condition. Sometimes, though, we can get to that particular pain point and we can start to move into freedom or wellness, only to realize that the cost was far higher than we'd anticipated. We find that there are unexpected consequences.

In John 5:5-6, Jesus confronts a long-time invalid:

A man was there who had been ill for thirty-eight years. When Jesus saw him lying there, and knew that he had already been a long time in that condition, He said to him, "Do you wish to get well?"

We often read that story and wonder why Jesus would ask such a seemingly obvious question. "Do you want to get well?" He asked. Most of us read that and think, *Well, duh, of course he wants to be well! Who would want to remain an invalid the rest of his life?* However, we don't often stop and think about all of the consequences of the invalid being healed. He would have to get a job. What was he qualified to do after 38 years as an invalid and beggar? Everyone who had ever known him had only known and related to him as a beggar and invalid. Now, they would have to get to know him all over again. What if they didn't like him as a healthy and whole man? His entire circle of acquaintances and friends might change. Being healthy, whole and, employed, he would then be solely responsible for himself and a household. He'd not done that for nearly four decades. What would that be like?

I believe this is why God often heals us and brings us out of bondage in stages. It's not that He never miraculously cures someone instantly because sometimes He does; most of the time, though, healing and freedom is a process and not an event. After God led the Israelites out of Egypt, He brought them to the Promised Land a year later. They weren't ready, so He kept them in the wilderness another 39 years and worked with them to properly prepare and test them for the blessing He wanted to give them. The Israelites hated being slaves to the Egyptians, and God heard their cries for freedom. Yet once they were out in the wilderness, free at last, what did they do? They started complaining and grumbling about how good they had it back in Egypt. Freedom wasn't as easy as they had thought; they weren't prepared for it to be hard. All they had ever known was bondage. They might have dreamt of freedom, but they couldn't really imagine what it would be like. They had no frame of reference for it.

This is true for us, as well. I think maybe it's because we approach healing and freedom with the wrong perspective. We tend to approach change as a way of escaping our current circumstances — as a means of running away from something. We desire a spouse because we are tired of being single, not because we fully understand what it means to participate in a healthy, God-centered marriage. We want to move out of our parents' house because we want to be free to do whatever we want, not because we have considered the responsibility of maintaining our own household and wisely decided to pursue that option. We dream about leading a ministry because it looks important and impressive, not because we have calculated the cost to our personal and professional life and deemed it worthy to follow God into His work.

I think we do the same with healing and freedom. I don't know how often we pursue freedom and healing because we have thought about, and are envisioning, our new life. More often than not, I believe we ask God for freedom and healing because we are tired of the old, not because we are excited about a vision of the new. The Israelites got caught in this trap. They didn't have a vision for freedom; they just knew they were tired of slaving away for the Egyptians. Initially, it was fear of being recaptured by the Egyptians that kept them moving, but once they were safe on the other side of the Red Sea, that was no longer enough motivation. There was no clear picture of their future to draw them along when things got hard. When God finally did give them a glimpse into the Promised Land, they retreated into fear, and it was that fear that kept them out for another 39 years.

I was so much like the Israelites when I first came back from Washington. I didn't know what freedom from Paul would look like; I was just desperate to get away from the stress and tension that characterized our marriage at the time. I wasn't running to anything as much as I was running away from something. Like the Israelites, I cried out to God and He heard me. He delivered me and led me into a wilderness season. Because it was a new experience for me, I spent a lot of time looking back over my shoulder, longing for the old and familiar even though it had been unhealthy. I developed selective amnesia and picked out the few positive moments as reasons for justifying my desire to return to the marriage. The wilderness was a hard road and I didn't yet have a picture of the future to draw me forward. What I did have was what the Israelites had: the presence of God leading me along, one day at a time. The Israelites had God in a pillar of cloud by day and a pillar of fire by night.[17] I had God in His Word and in the Holy Spirit residing in my heart.

God had to keep reminding me that He was a God of new things, not old. When I would turn my head back to look at my past, He would gently take my face and turn it back to Him and the future He had prepared. He would remind me of the following verse from Isaiah 43:18-19:

Behold, I will do something new, now it will spring forth; will you not be aware of it? I will even make a roadway in the wilderness, rivers in the desert.

Whenever I reached out to Paul in weak and lonely moments, shrouded in the illusion that things hadn't been so bad, God would clear the air with His Word and the truth of who Paul was. In my wilderness season, God nourished me and took care of every need. He showed me He could be trusted with my very life. The desert was my transition. It was where God changed my "running away from" mentality into a "walking forward into" mindset. It was where He helped me let go of Paul's infidelity and embrace His faithfulness. It was where He helped me let go of the lies of the world and embrace His truth.

It was where we dealt with my past, and it was where He began to give me a picture of my future.

Chapter 24

BLOOM WHERE YOU ARE PLANTED

Truly charity has no limit; for the love of God has been poured into our hearts by His Spirit dwelling in each one of us, calling us to a life of devotion and inviting us to bloom in the garden where He has planted and directing us to radiate the beauty and spread the fragrance of His Providence.-
St. Francis de Sales

The apostle Paul wrote letters to churches while imprisoned. John Bunyan wrote *Pilgrim's Progress* while imprisoned. Madame Guyon, a French mystic, wrote her biography while imprisoned. Exile and imprisonment, while uncomfortable, are often the most conducive environments for writing. In December 2012, while on vacation in Folsom, God opened the door to my own journey as one of His correspondents.

On December 31, during a church service at New Song, my pastor challenged the congregation with three questions: 1) What is the one thing you most desire from God?; 2) What is one thing you lack?; and 3) What is one thing you need to let go of? With the idea that less is more, we were asked to let God show us one thing in each area that we most needed to pray about and focus on in the coming year, instead of spreading ourselves thin trying to address every area of improvement in our lives.

After praying through the questions and journaling my answers, it occurred to me to build in some accountability and blog about my journey every day throughout 2013. I remember that it all happened very suddenly. One minute I was journaling; the next, I was sitting at the laptop banging out an introductory post, setting the stage for a year's worth of blogging. Now, as easily as writing had always come to me, perseverance had never been my strong suit. I had always been a good starter but a poor finisher. I lacked stamina. I had a blog site where I'd posted a number of entries, but there had been no rhyme or reason to the timing. I wrote as I felt led, and I sure never committed to any hard and fast schedules. But there I was that night, following God's lead and committing to 365 blog posts that were to start the next day—no preparation, no planning, and just one day of lead time.

It was better that way, really. If I'd had time to think about it, I probably would have talked myself out of the plan, or I would have analyzed it to death and bogged myself down in the details instead of just doing it. As it was, there was no time to put together an outline for the year or plan topics. It was just God saying "Go!" and me taking off and trusting Him to provide. That reality hit me square between the eyes the next morning. *What have I done*, I thought, *I don't have 365 blog entries in me*. That's when God reminded me that I wouldn't be writing the posts; He would. That little exchange turned into the first entry in the *One Thing* blog. One entry turned into two, two days turned into a week, and before I knew it, the first month was in the books. Week after week, and month after month, God was faithful to show up. For my part, I was faithful to just show up at my laptop each day and ask God what He wanted to write.

That year of writing provided tangible evidence of God's presence in my life. It is black and white proof that He is real and that He loves me. Those blog posts are mile markers I can go back to when my faith wavers and I begin to doubt. I can look back over the moments when He spoke to me, when He comforted me, when He encouraged me, when He fought for me, and when He provided for me. I can read about all the times He answered my prayers. I can see every time He took care of me.

Those entries were also cathartic. In January 2013, I stopped making trips up to Folsom and that meant an end to my counseling sessions, but God picked up where Ellen had left off. After 18 months of stripping away layers of junk, God would use that year to begin the painstaking work of rebuilding me into the woman He had always designed me to be. He would begin opening doors to His plans and purposes for my life and He would give me opportunities to practice things I'd learned – to trust and obey Him in greater measure.

In 2013, as I leaned in to the process of writing the *One Thing* blog, I continued to struggle in that season of stillness and solitude. I remained without a home church or small group in Orange County. I had entered the last few months of paying off my bills. I was no longer making trips up north to Folsom. I was far beyond the starting gate of my journey, and the finish line was nowhere in sight. It is tempting in that place to try and satisfy your own desires. This is where doubt and fear creep in and threaten to derail you. You wonder if God has forgotten about you and your dreams. You fear that God won't come through for you with anything good. You doubt that the season will ever end.

That's where a man named Achan got into trouble. In Joshua 7:16-26, we read about a man who disobeyed God and decided to satisfy his desires himself. After being told to not take any of the spoil from the raid on Jericho, Achan withheld a few pieces of gold and silver and hid them under his tent. He was eventually found out and he, along with his entire family, was killed as punishment. Just a few days later, the Israelites rout another city, Ai, and God allows them to keep the spoil from that raid. Achan didn't know how close he was to receiving treasure from God. Just a few more days and he would have received what he'd wanted.

We cannot know what God has planned for us. I had no idea that God was going to open up several doors of blessing for me in late 2013. In September, I made the last payment on my bills. That same month, I visited a church in Anaheim where Lee

Strobel was speaking and ended up finding a church home and a small group. Also in September, God led me to approach a coworker about praying together each week, and that turned into a small workplace prayer group, with three of us meeting each Thursday at lunch.

God's grace is like that—surprising, unexpected, and abundant. Where He rains it down, blessings spring up. His Word says that He is the One who makes streams in the desert and a roadway in the wilderness (**Isaiah 43:19**). He is the One who sends the rain and sun to grow us in the gardens where He has planted us. Our job is simply to remain there, rooted and grounded in His love.

I never had children of my own, but God has put quite a few young men and women in my life who have been like sons and daughters to me. He has used them to redeem the mistakes of my past and grow me in grace.

Most, if not all, of them have struggled with dating issues. It's difficult to be single in this world; society tells us that we shouldn't be. Just look at all of the online dating commercials on television and on the radio. The internet is no better. Very few of us know how to really make the most of our single years. We wish them away. We hunker down and sulk through them. We self-medicate with food, drink, and busyness. Some of us buy into the illusion that casual dating with sex is the way to survive until we meet "the one." Whichever coping mechanism we choose, all of us have one thing in common: we suffer from an identity crisis.

When we don't know who we are in Christ, we will exhaust ourselves looking to be someone in a relationship. When we don't have purpose and meaning in a relationship with Jesus, we will try to find fulfillment in dating. We were designed to worship someone or something, and if we are not worshiping God, we will make an idol of our body, or someone else's, and turn our bed into an altar.

The young people I've met have all believed lies — about God and about themselves. By God's grace and in His mercy, He has freed me from those lies and has given me countless opportunities to speak His truth into the lives of these young people. For one young woman, that meant telling her an unplanned pregnancy is not an accident. Life, however conceived, is an intentional act of God — a miracle and a gift from our Creator. For another woman, it meant encouraging her to not rush into another dating relationship after breaking up with her boyfriend. Rather, I suggested she spend some time alone with God, seeking His will for her life. For a young woman I worked with, God led me to spend time with her and her young son, adopting them as daughter and grandson for a time and coming alongside to support her journey as a single mom. Finally, for one young man who grew to be like a son to me, it meant praying with and for him, and mentoring him professionally and personally.

Offering counsel to young people is one thing; having them receive it and apply it is something else entirely. Sometimes, it seemed as though my words just went in one ear and out the other. Other times, I just got blank stares. On some occasions, I was flat-out rejected. As challenging as those mentoring relationships sometimes were, they served as an effective training ground for me. Allowing people to be who they are has never been a strong suit for me, especially in my marriages. I tended to be controlling, and nagged each husband to do things the way I thought they should be done. With these young people, I got the chance to practice accepting and loving them for who they were in that moment, and then taking my concerns directly to God and asking Him to change the things He desired to be different. I'll be honest, that's been a tough nut to crack in my life. Judgment and criticism love to rear their ugly heads, but God is changing my heart. He has been patient and gracious with me, and that's helped me to extend the same towards others.

In sharing my story with these men and women, I've begun to see value in all the heartache and brokenness of my life. There's been so much loss due to incredible folly, but the lessons are now available to other people who need them. There's encouragement and hope for them. They don't have to travel the same road that I did, but some will choose to do it anyway. They don't have to make the same mistakes that I did, though some will end up doing just that. It breaks my heart to see them ignore or avoid wise counsel, but then I remember that I did the exact same thing for nearly three decades. I have absolutely no room to criticize, so I pray instead. I ask God to give them wisdom and discernment, and to keep foolishness far from them. I speak purity and integrity over them. Mostly though, I ask God to give each of them the grace to see their need for Jesus as their Savior.

Chapter 25
PERSEVERANCE PAYS OFF

An assured part of God's pledged blessing to us is delay and suffering. A delay in Abram's own lifetime that seemed to put God's pledge beyond fulfillment was followed by seemingly unendurable delay of Abram's descendants. But it was only a delay: they "came out with great substance." The pledge was redeemed. God is going to test me with delays; and with the delays will come suffering, but through it all stands God's pledge: His new covenant with me in Christ, and His inviolable promise of every lesser blessing that I need. The delay and the suffering are part of the promised blessing; let me praise Him for them today; and let me wait on the Lord and be of good courage and he will strengthen my heart. – **C.G. Trumbull on Genesis 15:12-14**

As 2013 started to wind down, and God started to open doors to fellowship and service, I began to experience conflict. My hope and expectation had been that once I was debt-free, I would be able to return to Folsom, but that particular door remained firmly closed. There were no opportunities which led in that direction; instead, God seemed to be planting me even more deeply in Orange County. I was about to spend some time learning the difference between expectation and expectancy.

Expectations are internal and personal — the outcomes we desire in any given situation or relationship. They are a benchmark we lay out, and our response is determined by whether or not the actual outcomes match up with our desired outcomes. Expectancy is different. It is a general sense of hope and anticipation with no personal or specific agenda attached to it.

I had some very specific expectations as the year came to a close, but very little expectancy. I wanted what I wanted, and disappointment soon followed as I realized God wasn't moving me back to Folsom. At that point, I had a decision to make. I could continue as I had, with a "visitor" mentality, and remain on the outskirts of every part of my life. I could just bide my time and refuse to engage fully in my current circumstances. I could pout and sulk and wallow in self-pity because my expectations hadn't been met. Or, I could trade my expectations for expectancy. I could choose to jump into my circumstances with both feet — fully engaging in them with an expectant heart, alert for God's presence, power, and provision, regardless of if or when God chose to move me.

When my expectations of returning to Folsom weren't met, I had to adjust to the reality that I would be in Orange County a while longer. What would life be like at a new church? In a new small group? How would I make new friends? How would things go in a new prayer group at work? Would I click with my coworkers in the same way I had up north? Everything was unknown and uncomfortable, and I could feel fear tugging at my leg, tempting me to hang back and not move forward into these new circumstances.

It was a lot like when I was trying to decide whether or not to pursue the annulment for my third marriage. Moving into new territory — a life without Paul — was a frightening proposition, but one of the verses God put in front of me at that time was Hebrews 10:39: "But we are not of those who shrink back to destruction, but of those who have faith to the preserving of the soul." Playing small, shrinking back, and generally living from a place of fear never serves us well; neither does it honor God.

Ultimately, I chose to engage. I chose to step out in faith in all the areas where God seemed to be holding the door wide open. I started attending Eastside Christian Church in Anaheim each weekend, and I signed up for several of the orientation activities and classes they were offering at the time. I joined a small group and started meeting with them each week. I eventually started volunteering in the church's café two or three times each month. I stepped into a new role at work and took on new responsibilities. I began meeting each week with a couple of coworkers at lunch to pray and share life.

God blessed each of those steps of faith. He gave me courage and boldness to try new things and to get to know new people. Experiences which I couldn't imagine being as good or as satisfying as those I had known in Folsom turned out to be unexpectedly rich and wonderful.

The apostle Paul wrote in 1 Corinthians 2:9:

> *"Things which eye has not seen and ear has not heard, and which have not entered the heart of man, all that God has prepared for those who love Him."*

We cannot know, in seasons where it is difficult to persevere, the blessings God is preparing to give us. In my own life, there have been three specific occasions when I ended up on my knees before God during seasons where I wanted to give up. In each of those seasons, my perseverance paid off in surprising ways.

The first time, I wanted to quit my job. I was getting established in my relationship with God and things were becoming increasingly difficult at work. The more I pursued God, the more I saw the worldliness of my workplace and the less I wanted to be there. I wanted to quit and go into full-time ministry. If I had to guess, I'd say that most, if not all, new Christ-followers go through some kind of season where they feel like this. You're in the honeymoon phase with God, and you just want to be with Him all the time.

The second time, I wanted to quit my family. Being a new believer, I hadn't yet grown in grace enough to really accept them as they were. I was incredibly judgmental and critical, and I got to the point where I just wanted to wash my hands of them. I didn't want to spend time with them, I didn't want to meet them where they were in life, and I certainly didn't feel like loving them like Jesus.

The third time, I wanted to quit my church. I'd been visiting a different church in the area whose worship and teaching style were very different from that of New Song. After visiting a couple of times, I was ready to jump ship and start attending this new church based on an emotional response. There was no leading from God in His Word, or in any other way; I just wanted to follow my heart.

In all three instances, by the grace of God, I didn't act on my desire to quit. I took that desire to Him, on my knees, confessed my struggle and asked God to help me do the right and wise thing. In each case, He gave me the power to persevere and stay put. In each case, there was an incredible and unforeseen blessing waiting for me down the road.

At work, God gave me countless opportunities to share my faith and minister to young women. He opened the door to deep and abiding friendships through our workplace prayer group. One day, He set it on my heart to meet with every person in the office and tell them what I appreciated about them. God gave me a unique blessing for each of the 40 people I met with that day, but the real gift was for me. I got to witness transformation up close and personal as I watched each individual's face change from apprehension and uncertainty, wondering why they were being called in to a meeting, to gratitude and joy as God spoke encouragement, love, and hope into their lives. God let me experience just the tiniest fraction of the joy He gets from blessing us as His kids, and it's something I won't ever forget.

The blessing at church and with my family was a joint one. In one of New Song's sermons, we were encouraged to reconcile with someone we'd been experiencing conflict with for some time. God immediately put my brother-in-law on my mind. I knew there was a lot of bad blood between us, and I knew I'd have to hear a lot of difficult things from him about my behavior, but I knew without a doubt that God was calling me to meet with him. The next week, I arranged to have dinner with him. We spent four hours together that night, and as expected, many of the things he shared with me were painful to hear. God gave me the grace to endure it, and the humility to apologize and ask for his forgiveness. By the end of the evening, we had made our peace and I invited him, along with my sister and my mom, to New Song's Christmas Eve service where both my mom and sister invited Jesus to be their Savior.

At the end of 2013, as I stepped through the doors God was holding open, I couldn't anticipate the blessings He would bring. But in the same ways that He had been faithful with my family, work, and church life before, God continued to show up in mind-blowing ways, surprising me with His grace and goodness.

In our prayer group at work, we decided to get more intentional about praying for the lost. We began fasting our lunch when we met each week, asking God for more opportunities to share our faith and to grow our group as He saw fit. It took about four months, but God answered our prayers in a huge way. Within the span of about three weeks, God brought six new people to our group. The sudden growth forced us to put some structure to the time we spent together, and placed the three of us who had formed the group into leadership roles. We took turns leading the study discussions, and it gave each of us opportunities to stretch our teaching legs. For someone who never thought of herself as a public speaker, I was constantly surprised by how God loosened my tongue and opened my mouth to share His Word.

In my small group, God gave me new friendships and He encouraged me through them to be bolder as a leader in Bible study environments. Through that group, I was able to practice sharing pieces of my story, and through that experience, I really started to get a picture of just how much God had done in the years since bringing me back to California.

At work, my new job responsibilities partnered me up with the young man I mentioned earlier. God would end up giving me a year, and numerous opportunities, to mentor him. We would grow into close friends, staying in contact to this day. It was in the workplace where I would meet the young woman whose son would become my adopted grandson. My time with them would bring hours of joy as I indulged my inner grandma, a desire that had long been on my bucket list.

Perseverance pays off. Just ask Simeon and Anna. In Luke 2, we read about these two saints who lived lives of righteousness and faithfulness. In their advanced years, God blessed them by orchestrating circumstances so that they were able to behold the sight of Jesus when His parents brought Him to the temple in Jerusalem to dedicate Him to God.[18] We have no idea just how much God wants to bless us. We can fall into the trap of thinking that God is holding out on us, and that He wants us to live a life devoid of joy or pleasure. We struggle when life gets hard, and we want to quit. We can't imagine any kind of good outcome in our present pain. But just like the sun hidden above the clouds during a storm, God's blessings and joy await us beyond the struggles and trials. We may not be able to see them, but they're still there. When we persevere, we are rewarded with the sun break—the revelation that God has been with us the whole time and that He was worth the wait.

Chapter 26

THE HOME STRETCH

Christianity is less about cautiously avoiding sin than about courageously and actively doing God's work. The biggest mistake a man can make in life is to always be afraid of making a mistake. –**Dietrich Bonhoeffer**

The end of 2013 brought with it a question: What was next after a year of blogging? The opportunity God had given me in the *One Thing* blog had resulted in 365 entries, no small feat considering my poor track record when it came to sticking with things and seeing them through to the end. The fact that I had shown up at my laptop every single day for an entire year was nothing short of miraculous for someone like me.

I'd gotten used to the daily routine of writing with God. Every night during the work week, and every morning of the weekends, we would meet and collaborate. I didn't know what life would look like without that daily appointment. I wondered if 2013 would be it, or if God would open the door to another year's worth of blogging.

During the last few months of the year, as I began to ask God what was next, I felt like "fearlessness" was the word He gave me. Scriptures in my daily reading seemed to all point in that direction. One night, as I was driving home from church, it was almost comical how obvious God made it. On a huge neon billboard next to the freeway, a message came up just as I was driving by: the word "fearless" lit up the screen in huge block letters. Another day, the phrase "Year of No Fear" popped into my head.

It shouldn't have come as much of a surprise that God would have me write about fear; I've spent most of my life living from that place. I've been afraid to be noticed, and I've been afraid to go unnoticed. I've been afraid of failure and making mistakes, and I've been afraid of success. I've been afraid of commitments, and I've been afraid of remaining alone. If I could have made a living from being a professional fraidy-cat, I would have enjoyed monumental success.

When I lived in Folsom, just before I moved to Washington, I briefly lived a pretty fearless life. I had been following God into activities that looked pretty bold and outrageous from my perspective at the end of 2013. Looking back, I was amazed by the steps of faith I'd taken to lead others around Folsom looking for homeless men and women to feed, to spend time with women and children at a local transitional home, and to stand up on stage at church and promote all of it. It was so far beyond my comfort zone, yet there I was, following God into all of it.

That fearlessness didn't come from a confidence in my own abilities. I actually felt pretty inadequate to do what He was asking. I constantly questioned whether or not I was the right person for the job, but I never doubted that the tasks were important to God and that I was doing His work. That conviction is what propelled me forward and through my fear. I didn't worry about whether or not people would follow me; I was only concerned about following God into what He had prepared.

Three years later, though, in the aftermath of my mess with Paul, a new fear cropped up: I was afraid that I'd made too big of a mistake to ever be used again by God. I was afraid that I could never be trusted again. I'd broken the faith in a huge way, and in many respects I felt like John Mark when the apostle Paul refused to take him on a mission trip. John Mark had bailed on Paul and Barnabas during an earlier trip, and Paul was understandably reluctant to trust him again with such an important role.[19] Whenever I thought about the possibility of serving once again, shame and embarrassment would immediately rise to the surface and I'd chastise myself for thinking that I could ever be a useful and contributing member of God's family again. Fear of people knowing everything I'd been through, and judging me for it, bound up any hopes I entertained of being in ministry ever again.

That wasn't how God saw me, though. In June 2013, I made this entry in my journal: *Every mistake, every foolish decision, every poor choice… God redeems every bit of it and turns it into preparation for use in a particular mission field later in life. He prepares and then positions us to serve others… never think that your life is too broken for God to use. Your brokenness is the foundation for God's ministry through you.* Out of our mess, God crafts a message.

The blog posts that would come out of 2014's *Year of No Fear* would build on the *One Thing* entries, and would further help me to embrace my humanity and my past. God would help me work through more subtle fears in my life, like being afraid to take chances, being afraid to get close to people and trust again, and being afraid to live fully as He made me. I became bolder in sharing my story with others, and more confident in God and His love and grace for me.

God would spend 2014 showing me how He had shaped and gifted me. He would give me opportunities to practice using those gifts, and He would help me find and use my voice, both verbally and in writing.

One of the reasons the Israelites spent 40 years in the wilderness was so that a rebellious and unbelieving generation would die off. When God brought them to the edge of the Promised Land, instead of believing God's promise that He would establish them there, they shrank back in fear and started grumbling about how it would have been better had they died in Egypt or in the wilderness (Numbers 13 and 14). In Numbers 14:23, God gives His judgment: "Not one of them will ever see the land I promised on oath to their forefathers. No one who has treated me with contempt will ever see it." The Israelites would follow God through the desert for 40 years, and during that time every adult male 20 years and older would die off. An entire generation never got to leave the desert experience because they refused to believe and receive God's promise of something greater.

As 2014 opened, there were still a couple of areas of resistance in my life that I needed to surrender. One was an attitude; the other was a behavior. Both were connected to God having placed me in Orange County for yet another year.

I had spent two weeks at Christmas and New Year's in Folsom on vacation. When my vacation was nearing its end, I refused to say, "I'm going home." Orange County wasn't home, and I was adamant about not referring to it in that way. Now, that might seem like a really trivial thing, but it was indicative of a greater rebellion in my heart. Orange County *was* my home for the time being. It had been my home for the previous year, and it was going to be my home for the next year, regardless of whether or not I wanted to be there. Refusing to accept that fact put me in direct opposition to God, and that's not the position I wanted to be in with Him.

I'd also been dragging my feet with regard to my tithing. Because I hadn't found a home church in Orange County, I'd continued to send my tithe to New Song. After God opened the door to becoming a member at Eastside, I knew I should switch my tithing to them, but I hadn't. It had been three months, and I was attending regularly; my tithe belonged to my church home. There was that word again: *home*. It felt disloyal to call Eastside home and to move my tithe there, but I knew God was calling me to do just that. There was nothing actually disloyal about it. I was simply clinging to my past. I was being stubborn and rebellious. I felt like I had let go of so many other things and people. Why did I have to let go of that, too?

I'd lost so much in my life: special people, jobs, homes, possessions. Sometimes, in the face of tremendous losses, we get to a point where we decide enough is enough. We refuse to lose one more thing in our life. We can become over-protective of the little we still have, even if it's not good for us. If we're not careful, we can move beyond protecting what we have and we can cross the line into accumulating. In order to guarantee we don't lose anything more, we will try to fill the near emptiness with stuff. My roommate in Orange County sometimes watched the show "Hoarders," and I immediately noticed a pattern with the folks on the show. Their hoarding had all been precipitated by a significant loss in their life. They'd lost a job. They'd lost a loved one. They'd lost a relationship. They'd lost something or someone which had been dear to them and they'd not dealt with it in a healthy way. Instead, they spent the rest of their life attempting to fill the hole that loss had created.

After more than two years in the wilderness and having been stripped of so much, I was tired of loss. I was tired of being emptied out. God had begun to refill my life in certain areas at the end of 2013, and I was caught up short when faced with the prospect of going backwards for a moment to let go of my attitudes about home and tithing. That, however, is the nature of our relationship with God. He empties and He refills. He gives and He takes away. When we let Him, He continually evaluates us and makes adjustments. As He has new things to give us, He helps us make room for those things. Sometimes, it's material wealth. Other times, it's relationships and people. Yet other times, it's our attitudes and behaviors. It's called sanctification, and it's the daily process of getting rid of the things of self to make room the things of God. In His economy, every day has the potential to be a spring cleaning day.

In January 2014, God went through my spiritual closet and held up my attitudes about home and tithing, letting me know it was time for them to go. It was like giving up two of my favorite pieces of clothing. They'd grown so comfortable over time and I loved wearing them. It was difficult parting with them, but part I did. I let New Song know that I'd found a new church home and that I would be switching over my tithing the following month. They would always be my first church home, the church in which I'd become a believer and where I'd grown up in my faith. Nothing could ever change that, no matter where I or my tithe went. It had been prideful of me to think that I knew better than God where my tithe belonged. He knew long before I did that I would make this transition, and He had already prepared both churches. I had to trust in His provision on both fronts. In Orange County, I settled in to life and embraced the things I enjoyed about being there, laughing at myself when I started to say and do things like the locals. I didn't know exactly how much more time I had in Orange County, but for whatever time I had down there, it was home.

July 17, 2014. It had been a hectic morning at work. When I ran out to grab some lunch, my head was still spinning with the tasks that were piled on my plate. The last thing I expected was to be chatted up by the guy in front of me as I waited in line at the

Subway sandwich shop. Even more unexpected was his request for my phone number and an invitation to have lunch with him. Most unexpected of all was my response after I gave him my number and went back to my car.

That day in July was both a test and graduation of sorts. It had been flattering to be noticed, and it would have been so easy to accept the lunch invitation. After all, I hadn't been on a date in almost three years; some people might have said that I was entitled to a little fun. While it's true that going on a lunch date wouldn't have been a sin, the test was in the process I went through to make my decision. Was I going to respond as I had when I met Paul? Was I the same person I had been back then? What kind of fruit had my years in the wilderness produced?

Four years earlier, almost to the day, I had been matched up with Paul on eHarmony, and a week later he was professing his love for me. Thinking I had it all together, I launched myself full speed into a relationship with him. But that afternoon in July was different. I went back to my car, closed the door, and bowed my head to pray. Knowing now that I *didn't* have it all together, I exercised caution and asked God for wisdom and discernment. In the days following that lunch invitation, I received several text messages and a phone call from my would-be suitor. Premature and inappropriate expressions of affection, along with other indications of neediness, immediately sent up red flags in my mind. Things that attracted me four years earlier now repelled my interest.

When I met Paul, I leaned heavily upon my own understanding and my broken experiences with men who were unchurched and rejecting Christ. This time around, I had a foundation of God's Word and first-hand observation of godly men to guide my decision-making. With Paul, I had no boundaries and no real sense of who I was or what was acceptable to me. I had been willing to accept bad behavior and settle for less than God's best for me. This time around, I was quick to recognize warning signs based on who God said I was and what He desired for me. I had four years of journaling under my belt—a body of work representing my efforts to understand my past and learn from it.

Later that day, as I drove to the gym and heard God whisper to me that I was no longer anyone's mistress, I felt like He was showing me "before" and "after" pictures, but it wasn't superficial changes that we were celebrating. God had changed me from the inside out. He had renewed my mind. He had given me a new heart. "This is who you used to be," He was saying, "and this is who you are now." I had been given an extreme makeover in the years since God had brought me back from Washington, and that day in July was a "big reveal" moment for me.

When we've gone through significant change in our life over a long period of time, we can sometimes become oblivious to just how different we are. As we see ourselves every day, the changes are imperceptible to us. It's not until we see a side-by-side comparison that the enormity of the change hits us. When God does this, it's not to puff us up with pride; rather, it is to glorify Himself. In the enormity of our change, we see the expansive and infinite power and grace of God. We see the reality of Jeremiah 32:27, "Behold, I am the Lord, the God of all flesh; is anything too difficult for Me?"

Chapter 27

WE ALL HAVE A STORY TO TELL

The gifts we receive here are all part of our preparation for eternity. If we are faithful with the little we are given here, God promises that we will be given much more in heaven. The gifts we are given here are both a test and a trust. God tests our hearts, our motives and our beliefs with these gifts. And, God tests our trustworthiness in this life to gauge what He will be able to give us in the next. – **Journal entry, August 2013**

From everyone who has been given much, much will be required; and to whom they entrusted much, of him they will ask all the more. – **Luke 12:48** n early 2012, during one of my trips to Folsom, I spent a few hours in a thrift store. I love thrift shops. I could easily spend an entire day going from one store to another, just browsing and losing myself in the odd collection of furniture, books, and trinkets that others have discarded. I've found many a bargain in secondhand stores, including London Fog jackets and Steve Madden shoes. If you're willing to put in the time to search the racks and shelves, there are wonderful treasures to be found.

On this particular trip, I was in the mood for books. Usually, I stay out of the book aisles. First, I always have a stack of books waiting in my "to be read" pile and I never need to add to it. Second, they're bulky and heavy to store and move. That's probably why so many books end up in the thrift shop. Nevertheless, that's where I found myself, head tilted to the right, trying to read the titles along the spine of each book. I wasn't sure what I wanted, but I figured I'd know it when I saw it.

I recognized the author's name first—Ruth Graham, daughter of Reverend Billy Graham. *Hmm,* I thought, *that might prove interesting reading.* I opened the book and scanned the inside jacket panels to read the teaser comments: "WHEN LIFE'S ROSY DREAMS DISSOLVE INTO DIFFICULT REALITIES

THAT BREAK OUR HEARTS, GOD SHOWS THAT
HE SPECIALIZES IN RESTORATION. If in these
pages you see your own life's experience mirrored in
our daughter's, may you, too, find a personal relationship with the same heavenly Father who continues
to be her strength, comfort, and joy." "For any who
have experienced the tragedy of infidelity and wrong
choices, Ruth unfolds her life, showing that the grace
of God is sufficient." "By sharing openly from her
own experiences of heartache and by offering practical insights founded on biblical truth, Ruth Graham
has provided a resource that both equips us to pursue
wholeness and leads us into the arms of the only One
who can make us whole."

I hadn't even flipped through the introduction, but
something told me this was a book I needed to read.
I pulled the book off the shelf and continued looking.
Nothing came close to capturing my interest as much
as the book I held in my hands, *In Every Pew Sits a
Broken Heart: Hope for the Hurting*.[20] My own dream of
happily ever after had been shattered in Washington,
and it had come at the hands of an adulterous situation. In God's economy, there are no coincidences.
There was something God wanted to tell me through
this book, and as I took my treasure up to the register
to check out, I grew anxious to know what it was.

I finished the book in a matter of days; I couldn't put it down. The whole time I kept thinking, *She's writing my story.* She knew and understood the pain and shock of discovering a spouse's infidelity. She perfectly described the internal struggle between wanting to be forgiving and loving, and needing to be angry. She shared Bible verses which had sustained her, and many of those same Scriptures graced the pages of my own journals. Hers was a kindred spirit, one who had walked in similar shoes on a similar path. Like me, she was a woman who had not only suffered the end of a marriage due to lies and deceit, but she had also rushed into a subsequent marriage.

I wasn't the only one, I thought. Her story gave me hope. I read about her struggles and felt my own begin to lighten. Her brokenness spoke to mine. Ruth Graham had found grace, healing and forgiveness in her own wilderness seasons. Through her story, grace, healing and forgiveness found me.

Revelation 12:11 says that our accuser, Satan, will be overcome "because of the blood of the Lamb and because of the word of their testimony." In 2 Corinthians 1:4, we read that God:

> *...comforts us in all our affliction so that we will be able to comfort those who are in any affliction*

with the comfort with which we ourselves are comforted by God.

In verse 6, we are told that if we are afflicted:

...it is for your comfort and salvation; or if we are comforted, it is for your comfort, which is effective in the patient enduring of the same sufferings which we also suffer.

There is power in our affliction, and in the comfort God brings us, but only when we share our story — the power is in our testimony.

When we are willing to be vulnerable before others and tell of our struggles, our weaknesses, and our addictions, God takes that brokenness and turns it into a blessing. He redeems all that was meant for our destruction and He uses it to encourage and give hope to others who desperately need it. When we find grace and healing in the wilderness, we are to share it with others. When God grows us in wisdom and discernment, we are to pass it along. We are saved, healed, and delivered so that our stories might reveal that much more of God and the kingdom of heaven here in the world.

That is why I have such confidence that God will use this story — my story — for His glory. It is why I have hope that He will heal and deliver a good friend of mine who is working through her own addiction issues. She has shared with me that my story is her story, much like I felt as I read Ruth Graham's book. I believe that God will do a similar work in her life because I was once comforted and encouraged in the same way I have tried to comfort and encourage my friend.

As I was going through my journals, I found an excerpt from an email sent to me by a long-time friend when I was in the midst of some of the lowest and most frustrating seasons of my own journey. She had shared Exodus 15:26 with me and part of a devotional she was studying: *The word for heal means to mend (by stitching – ouch), repair thoroughly, make whole. The author writes, "I picture God focusing steadily on the object of repair. One stitch follows another. It takes time. I picture painful penetrations of the healing needle… I don't know about you, but I'm quite sure if my healing process had been painless, I would have relapsed."* She closed the note with her own encouragement to me: *Your Lord is with you, Joanna. He loves you. He has come to heal you and to set you free. Let Him be your portion. Let Him be your strength. Let Him fill your cup – He will make it overflow.*

God wastes nothing. He redeems it all. A life of pain, suffering, and affliction can be a glorious instrument of healing in the world, but we must steward well that which God allows into our life. We must be willing to endure the wilderness seasons and lean into them. We must be willing to let go of the "why" and embrace the "Who." For when we emerge from the test, we will go forth with a testimony – a powerful and effective weapon against the things that keep others bound up and imprisoned.

We are not to stay quiet, friends. We each have a story to tell. We are living, breathing testimonies of God's goodness and grace. Do not remain silent any longer! There are people in this world who need to hear your story. They need to know they are not alone in their suffering. They need to know there is hope for their hurt. They need to be encouraged to persevere through their trials.

They need Jesus. The only way some of them will ever meet Him may just be through *your* story.

ABOUT THE AUTHOR

A self-professed "geek for God," Joanna has been a follower of Christ since 2007, and is passionate about sharing God's Word and truth with the world. In 2013, she felt God prompting her to begin a daily blog, and she has been writing about her personal relationship with Jesus ever since. When she's not working or writing, she enjoys visiting thrift shops, sightseeing, watching movies, and taking in the occasional baseball or ice hockey game. You can follow her blog, Geek Speak, at http://gek4god.blogspot.com.

ENDNOTES

Introduction
1. 1 Samuel 16:7
2. Jeremiah 33:3

CHAPTER 1
3. Ephesians 4:26-27

CHAPTER 2
4. Rick Warren, "You Are Not An Accident," *The Purpose Driven Life* (Grand Rapids: Zondervan, 2002), 30-35

CHAPTER 5
5. Ephesians 5:33
6. Luke 7:47
7. John 10:10

CHAPTER 6
8. Barbara Wilson, *The Invisible Bond: How to Break Free from Your Sexual Past* (New York: Random House, 2006), 32-34

CHAPTER 9
9.   2 Samuel 12:24

CHAPTER 11
10.   Forrest Gump, dir. by Robert Zemeckis (1994)

CHAPTER 17
11.   "Noël," December 20, 2000 episode of *The West Wing* (NBC, 1999-2006)

CHAPTER 18
12.   1 Samuel 21-31
13.   1 Peter 1:16

CHAPTER 20
14.   Wilson, *Invisible Bond*
15.   1 John 1:9

CHAPTER 22
16.   1 Kings 19:12

CHAPTER 23
17.   Exodus 13:21

CHAPTER 25
18.   Luke 2:21-38

CHAPTER 26
19.   Acts 15:37-38

CHAPTER 27
20.   Ruth Graham, *In Every Pew Sits A Broken Heart: Hope For The Hurting* (Grand Rapids: Zondervan, 2004)

CPSIA information can be obtained
at www.ICGtesting.com
Printed in the USA
FSOW04n0758030317
31490FS